HOW TO SEDUCE A MAN

THE RIGHT WAY

3 Manuscripts in 1 Book, Including: How to Attract Men, How to Flirt and How to Influence People

Dean Mack

More by Dean Mack

Discover all books from the Social Skills Best Seller Series by Dean Mack at:

bit.ly/dean-mack

Book 1: *How to Flirt*

Book 2: *How to Start a Conversation*

Book 3: *How to Talk to People*

Book 4: *How to Ask Questions*

Book 5: *How to Be Funny*

Book 6: *How to Influence People*

Book 7: *How to Attract Men*

Book 8: *How to Attract Women*

Themed book bundles available at discounted prices:

bit.ly/dean-mack

Table of Contents

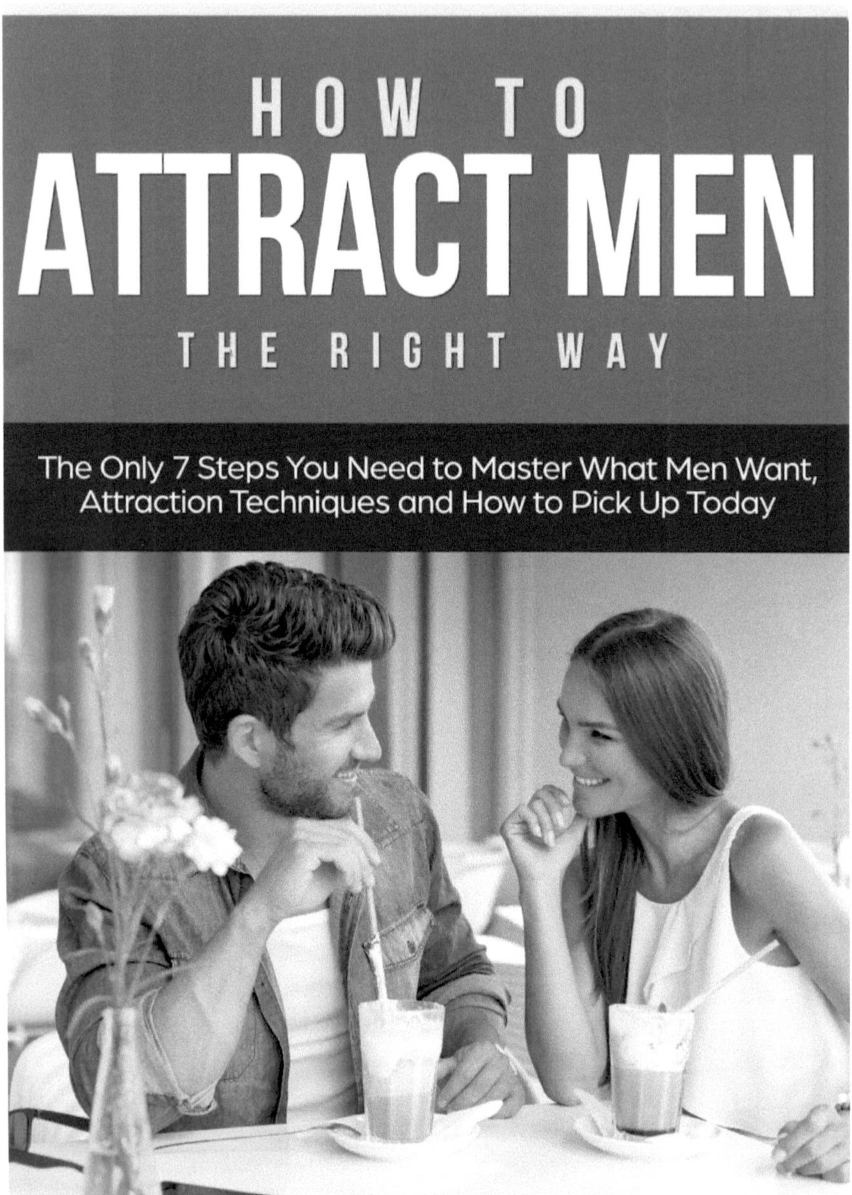
HOW TO
ATTRACT MEN
THE RIGHT WAY
The Only 7 Steps You Need to Master What Men Want, Attraction Techniques and How to Pick Up Today
DEAN MACK

BOOK 1: HOW TO ATTRACT MEN

THE RIGHT WAY

The Only 7 Steps You Need to Master What Men Want, Attraction Techniques and How to Pick Up Today

Dean Mack

Table of Contents

Introduction

Are you having trouble attracting the man of your dreams? Do you want to be the ultimate man magnet who always gets the most attractive, intelligent, successful, and understanding men? There's a piece of good news and bad news – the bad news is that there is not shortcut to getting the best men.

The good news, however, is that it isn't an impossible task. A man's brain is wired differently from a woman's. The psyche, thoughts, and emotions are all processed differently. Their minds are mapped differently, and any success with getting the best men begins by unlocking the secret to reading/understanding their mind.

Many thoughts, feelings, and situations will be interpreted in dramatically different ways because of the differences in the way men and woman think. When you have the key to understanding what exactly a man seeks, your chances of attracting their attention and forming fulfilling relationships increases. You get a considerable edge over others who don't understand the secret to unlocking their way through a man's heart. When you know practical, workable and effective solutions to make your way into a man's heart, it doesn't stop you from getting any man you want.

There are complex dynamics involved in the evolution of the human species, which helps you put together the puzzle of what a man truly wants in a woman. There are multiple evolutionary, psychological and neurological secrets involved in attracting the right man. Use these scientific secrets to your advantage by understanding precisely what a man wants.

For example, as a lady, won't you be more attracted to a man who is positive, healthy and boasts of healthy testosterone levels? Now, throw in a pleasantly charming personality, affectionate nature, chivalry, and a dazzling sense of humor. Wouldn't you really be attracted to a man who can be your knight in shining armor to look after you? From primordial ages, men have been hunters and gatherers, who've collected food for their family and protected them from the dangers of the jungle. This explains why until today our brains are wired to be attracted to men who are good providers and protectors. Now add to this primitive behavior the fundamental contemporary dynamics, where roles are easily interchangeable. This makes the relationship between men and women even more complicated.

Seduction, flirting and picking up isn't any less than a game, and to master any game, you need to learn its rules. I'll let you in on the secret rules, strategies and cheat-sheets involved to ace this game.

Similarly, based on the way their minds are mapped, men find certain traits highly attractive in a woman.

What you believe to be plain bad luck or lack of social skills when it comes to dating may simply be sending the wrong signals or aura that sends men away. Sometimes, without even without realizing it, we transmit the wrong vibes to people, which totally ruins our chances of enjoying fulfilling relationships.

How many times have you unfortunately wondered that a man is absolutely not in your league or totally unattainable? No one is outside your league. You can get any man you want if you have the confidence, self-belief and of course, a few amazing tricks up your sleeve. You have to tap into his subconscious mind to understand him and draw him closer to you. Yes, of course, a red lipstick, a sexy tank top, stilettos and a gorgeous smile helps, but it is all a mind game at the end of the day. If you are able to sway their subconscious mind in the right direction, you'll have them eating straight out of your palms.

The secret to making your way into a man's heart is by appealing and talking to his mind. When his subconscious mind views you as desirable, seducing, flirting and picking him up becomes a cakewalk.

There's a huge difference between men checking you out and men who just cannot keep away from your spell. Yes, the sheer magnetism where a guy can resist succumbing to your charm. This is exactly why realms of paper are being dedicated to research about attracting the opposite sex. We don't simply want men gaping at us, we want men who are hooked to us.

In the next few chapters, I will offer you the ultimate secrets for attracting the man you desire using practical and actionable tips that work in the real world. These are a combination of scientific, psychological, evolutionary and perfectly common sense tips that will open up a whole new world of dating and attracting men to you.

Chapter One -Step One: The Body Language of Seduction

For starters, conversation, pickup lines and texts can wait! Body language is the unsung superstar of dating. It isn't as much about what you are actually thinking or conveying. It's about how to make it positive enough for the other person to perceive it in a manner you intend.

Imagine having a superpower or secret weapon that can help you communicate your deepest thoughts, feelings and emotions without having to use a single word. Well, body language is indeed that superpower that helps you manipulate how others perceive you.

Research has revealed that people recall only 10 percent of the information that is passed on to them verbally and about 20 percent of the information communicated visually. However, when both verbal and nonverbal communication is combined, a staggering 80 percent of the message is absorbed.

When we keep our body language in a particular manner, we not just lead others to perceive what we want them to, but also trick our subconscious mind into believing its truth. So when you stand all tall and erect, you are actually leading your subconscious mind into believing that you are actually important and confident. The subconscious mind then directs out body to behave in a matching confident and self-assured manner. Let's just call it a little mind game you're playing with your subconscious mind.

If you combine both orally and visually communicated information, 80 percent of the information is retained.

For instance, if you want to reveal yourself as a sexy, confident seductress, your body language should help the other person perceive it without any trouble. Basically, if you're giving the wrong signals, the person will just not get it. So how does one give out the right message? Here's unlocking some of the most powerful body language secrets.

1. Smile

There are some universal gestures of acceptance and interest, and smile tops that list. You meet someone nice you truly into or interested in, shake hands, get their name, use the name and greet them with their name and finally, flash your most dazzling, hypnotizing smile. There's nothing more irresistible than a woman giving a warm, affectionate and confident smile that says, "I am ready if you are".

2. The Belly Button Rule

Your belly button should ideally face the individual you're truly attracted to. Even if you are facing the person or in another direction while talking to him, change your position to keep your belly button straight in front of the man you are interested in or addressing. It sends out a sort of subconscious message that you are totally into him, and focusing all your attention (including the body) in their direction. It works at a very primordial level. Try it!

3. The Magic Touch

Touch is the cornerstone of the dating and mating game. Even a slight touch can communicate intimacy and increase one's heart rates. It may not be a good idea to grab a man by his arm the moment you are introduced to him. However, a few flirtatious or gentle touches around a man's wrist or arm can do you a whole lot of good. This is a good first or second date strategy. Keep the frequency at a minimum of five times for every 15 minutes.

4. Stand in the Center of a Group

So if you are really looking to attract a man, stand smack in the center of your pack. You are more likely to be spotted and subconsciously viewed as a leader of the pack if you are standing in the middle rather than the outskirts. Even if you are not straightaway standing in the center, make your way into the center subtly. You are literally having yourself framed or flanked by others, and making it appear like you are the group's influencer. Hey, and who doesn't love leaders and influencers? Also, the human eyes are naturally drawn to people who are in the center of a space as that becomes the point of focus.

5. The Posture

Don't look hunched over that phone. Put it away now. That's not the best way to attract the attention of the man you want. Did you hear about Amy Cuddy's TED Talk research where she reveals that once you're bent, the body's cortisol level rise and testosterone level lowers? Yes, that's right. The moment you hunch, the body's stress hormones increase dramatically. No, that certainly doesn't mean you walk in with an obvious power pose or worse, exaggerated swag.

Maintain a subtle power pose by standing with your arms on the hips. The feet should ideally be about six inches away. According to research conducted by Cuddy, adopting a subtle power pose can reduce your stress level and increases testosterone levels, and make you feel even more confident and positive.

Now, why not use body language and posture to display your most flattering physical attributes? Notice how some women look amazing when they pull back their neck and shoulders and stand with their breasts out? If you have long legs, stand tall and keep ramp like sideway leg posture to demonstrate a sexy pair of legs. Reveal your best and most flattering attributes.

Sit up straight or lean back to appear more confident and flaunt your most attractive physical attributes. Want to make your butt look amazing? Arch your back and throw your shoulders behind. Bonus points if you're wearing a foxy, sexy pair of stilettos.

6. Use Hands, Duh!

One of the most effective ways to attract men is to use your hand generously, and not in the way you're thinking yet! Hint romantic actions and activities through hand gestures. It could be anything from caressing yourself to gently tapping your chest to touching your face or legs. There's no harm in dropping a little hint or being suggestive/flirtatious.

It communicates two things –something you'd like to do to the man or something that you'd like the man to do to you. If you're really creative, you can also use a bunch of props or objects to communicate the same thing. Some objects you can use include drink glasses and cigarettes. Subtle fidgeting will send powerful signals to the object of your desire about what you intend to do with them or that you have your eyes firmly fixated on them.

7. Let Your Lips Do the Talking

So what should be your first move when it's time to take control of wooing the man of your dreams? Your lips are the best 'go for the kill' weapons. Start talking to the man of your dreams. Now here's the trick, and this has to be done very subtly. Gently lick, purse or bite your lips. The lip movement should be noticeable without being in your face. You may already be doing this subconsciously. However, now be more mindful of it. Start doing it frequently while talking to the man you desire.

When you're eating, ensure you are doing it gradually, mindfully and intentionally. They will just not be able to resist your lip movements and will start sending cushy, romantic signals right back. Woohoo, you've scored a point!

8. Let Your Expressions Do the Trick

A majority of the time we think our facial expressions are a result of our subconscious actions that we have little control over. That may not be very true. If you read and learn more about body language, you realize that it can be manipulated to help the other person perceive a certain feeling or thought on a subconscious level.

Keep your expressions more engaging, involved and dramatic. Ensure you nod periodically (but not frequently enough to appear too eager to please) when the man of your dream is speaking to you. Appear enthusiastic and interested in what they are speaking. Acknowledge what they are saying with matching expressions or a nod. I'll give you a few killer tips to appear excited and interested while having a conversation with that special someone. Slowly lift your eyebrows, make consistent eye contact (yes more on this later) and mirror his expressions. It will help him connect with you on a subconscious level.

9. Mirror His Actions

As discussed in the earlier point mirroring a person's expressions, gestures, posture and body language works brilliantly on a subconscious level. Going back to evolutionary science, we instantly take to people who seem to belong to our type or kind. It had existed since primitive times when humans aped each other's actions to demonstrate their loyalty or belongingness for their tribe or group. It is referred to as a sense of affiliation in psychology, which is nothing but the motivation to belong to a certain group around us.

Today, when you mirror a person's gestures, expressions, and other body language, they receive subconscious signals that you are 'one among them,' which makes them take an instant liking for you. Be careful, however, that you don't overdo it or it will appear like you are imitating the man or worse, making fun of him. That's the last thing you want.

Keep it classy and subtle. You can hold your wine glass the way he has held his. Sip on your drink right after he takes a sip of his drink. Lean a little ahead if you find him leaning ahead while talking to you. If he is leaning against a wall, follow suit and lean subtly against a wall. Try and listen to the words he uses during the conversation very intently. Use the same words in your conversation to make yourself appear more and more like him.

Again, be discreet while mirroring his actions or you'll come across as too eager to please or without a mind of your own. Mirror his actions judiciously, but also retain your individuality.

10. Throw in Eye Contact

Of course, in the business world, continuous eye contact can be intimidating and unnerving. You'll be left wondering why the hell your associate or boss is giving you such intense looks. However, in social relationships, it works slightly differently. It conveys a sense of intimacy, interest, and attraction. It shows you are truly excited about meeting him and eager to know more about him.

Want to cast an even more effective spell on the man of your dreams? Combine meaningful eye-contact with occasional touches. Also, keep darting your eyes at his lips once in a while. It works like a charm!

My favorite tip is to combine eye contact and to lean a little forward while talking to him simultaneously. Attempt to get a little closer. If you both are seated, gently brush your leg against his without making it look forced or awkward. Another thing I often suggest is throwing your arms on the table if he is seated across the table from you. Let your arms accidentally brush against his hand.

Chapter Two - Step Two: Secrets of Dating Online

If you one of those women who is very confident of approaching Mr. Perfect in person, there's hope online. Now that we book everything from airline tickets to restaurant tables on the internet, why should it stop you from finding love online? It is a wonderful way to meet new people from varied backgrounds. Also, you establish a connection with people who share similar interests, hobbies and goals. Don't even get me started with the umpteen flirting and seduction opportunities. Yes, it's a minefield of men if you just know how to snag the most desirable ones.

Though online dating has munificent advantages, it has a downside too. There are thousands of profiles out there, and you've got it to really stand out to be noticed.Plus, there are the scams and fake profiles. How then do you make your profile and virtual persona interesting from others? Fret not, I've got you covered there. There are some neat tricks up my sleeve that works like a charm on a range of dating sites.

1. Create a Wow Profile

Even if you don't want to create a detailed and elaborate profile (though creating one will increase your chances of success), you should have a minimum of one profile picture and some fundamental details. I'll show you some secret tips for creating an attractive and well-optimized dating profile that attracts a swarm of desirable men.

For starters, always use a current profile picture. Men don't want to see how you looked 10 winters ago when you were several stones lighter. They want to see your real, honest self now. Tell me, wouldn't you be big time annoyed a guy put up a profile picture when he had a massive crop of hair on his head only to find him semi-bald when you meet? That's deception, and no one appreciates it!

Avoid using heavily filtered or doctored images. They may look great on your Instagram feed but don't belong on a dating profile. Try to keep it attractive, flirty and naughty, yet real. Quick tip: research has revealed that wearing red in your display picture helps you look more desirable. Reach out for your best red outfit in the wardrobe and go click happy! Of course, you can keep it a little revealing, sexy and flirtatious. Wear a nice dress with a flattering neckline.

Your picture probably speaks more than the written introduction. There's a lot that can be read from your posture and expression. Look your flattering best minus the deception. Opt for images that highlight your best features (everything from your gorgeous mane to dimpled smile to big eyes). Again, avoid making insanely seductive or provocative expressions. It doesn't really make you come across as classy and smart. Duck faces and pouts belong to Snapchat, avoid them here like the plague.

If you have a bunch of professionally shot pictures, I would strongly recommend using them as the extra images and not your main profile picture. Use pictures that show you in a more real and natural manner as your display picture.

You'll have the option of adding several supplementary images. Use this for adding images in different settings and from varied angles. It will offer a greater range to your persona. Add pictures that reveal your interests such as camping, fishing, playing tennis. They make you come across as a multidimensional person, who has a variety of passions. Keep the count of your supplementary images limited to 10.

2. Write a Power Packed Introduction

Ensure you mention all interests clearly, and above all don't forget to be witty, creative and original. No one likes to read hackneyed introductions about how you love meeting new people or what a romantic person you are. For example, don't simply say you love going skiing. Mention your most exciting skiing experience ever. This makes you more fun and sexier.

Similarly, everyone talks about how crazy they are about food. Write about the best meal you ever had or a memorable traditional feast you enjoyed in any part of the world. Make it seductive, specific and highly descriptive by adding details. There are a million profiles that say they love listening to music. Instead, mention the kind of music you like listening to. It gives the man who approaches you more substance or ground to start the virtual conversation.

Brag a bit but don't go overboard. Don't say you are smoking hot; let your images do the talking. Similarly, don't underplay yourself. Modesty is not a trait that'll win you many virtual admirers. Be your natural, flirty and fun self. Include a few cleverly suggestive phrases in your introduction without making it tacky.

Now, your life may have been an interesting soap opera but mentioning it here doesn't fulfill any purpose. There's no need to mention past affairs or relationships gone awry. Nix the drama, and don't present yourself as a desperate attention-seeking wimp. Men don't want drama queens. They are looking for a fun, sexy and confident woman who can take care of her emotions without appearing insecure and attention-seeking. Golden rule – never ever reveal confidential or highly personal details about yourself or your past until you can trust the person.

Also, don't make your profile an elaborate grocery list. I want someone who has the perfect large, black eyes, flattering height, Harvard graduate and more. It just makes you come across as a digger who is highly demanding and controlling. Don't make it obvious that you are looking for someone like an ex-lover. While it's alright to say you want someone fun and presentable, it isn't really wise to say you only want someone who has brown eyes, brown hair and is 5'11 inches tall.

3. Go for the Kill

Don't just set up a profile, wait for men to approach you, and then go on a replying spree. Be confident and proactive when it comes to approaching men. Quick tip: Bumble.com is a dating site where only women can approach men and not vice-versa. So, the rules are changing.

Increase your chances of getting the men you fancy by approaching them confidently. A great way to begin is by asking more open-ended questions or offering constructive comments about what's written in their profile.

You really don't have to draft Shakespeare style love notes to reveal your evolved writing skills. Write a short and snappy introduction by sounding real and natural. I know a lot of dating gurus say wait for a while before replying to someone who approaches you. Nah! It doesn't work in the fast-paced virtual dating field. People don't like to wait too much.

4. Stay Safe

First things first, no one should make you do anything that you aren't happy doing. It is alright to be clear and state upfront that you are not comfortable doing certain things or have certain dating rules.

For instance, some women don't like sharing their contact number immediately, which is a good practice. They prefer communication over a series of emails before actually talking over the phone. There are several ways to keep in touch via video chats and messengers, before meeting the man. Do what makes you comfortable. There are no rules. You make your own rules to do to safeguard your privacy. Build excitement and anticipation in the run-up to your meeting. The guy should be dying to see who you are! Use light flirting to make the wait even more exciting!

Be alert, cautious and watch out for signs that don't quite feel right. It is your responsibility to look after your safety and protect your privacy.

Always insist on picking a public place that is fairly crowded for your first meeting. As far as possible, avoid meeting someone for the first time near your residence or place of work. Similarly, I always advise women to share the contact details of their date along with the venue with a trusted friend, co-worker or family member.

Carry some non-dangerous tools like a pepper spray for safety on your first date, and always remember to split the bill. Don't come across as a gold digger who is only out to have a good time at the man's expense. It isn't very attractive for most guys trust me. Women who don't accept any obligation or favors, and come across as more independent are self-respecting can be insanely sexy for a man. Hold your head high and pick up your own tab instead of expecting the man to feed you. For the first date, don't make it an expensive affair. You don't really need a Michelin restaurant. Keep it no frills, comfortable and casual, where you can actually enjoy a conversation.

Nowadays, new agers opt for plenty of fun, offbeat activities, such as mountain climbing, cycling, and museum trips. Get to know each other, while doing fun activities together seems to be the mantra.

5. The First Date

Sit in a way that makes you come across as close to him as well as approachable. Opt for a seat where he can lay his eyes on you as soon as he enters. Be playful with hair, throw a suggestive glance in his direction and talk to someone who is near him in your sexiest voice to grab his attention without directly addressing him. Ensure again that you do it subtly and don't come across as a desperate attention seeker.

This works wonders if you do it exactly as it's intended to be done. Once every few minutes, find something that keeps you looking slightly busy. It can be browsing on your phone or a leaflet/menu. Appear a little unavailable. When you look at him, he's most likely gazing in your direction. Return his gaze. Maintain eye contact for a couple of seconds, followed by soft blinking of the eyes and flashing your best smile. Then, look away. This will make him want to start a conversation right away to know more about you.

Some guys don't like breaking the ice or making the first move. Don't be shy about taking the lead here and make your first move. Simply go up to him or if he comes up to you, make eye contact and say a courteous hello. Next, ask him an open-ended question or pay him a nice compliment. Go ahead and offer a brief introduction. Keep the questions uncomplicated and interesting. What dish would you highly recommend at this eatery? Keep compliments understated, cool and casual. However, make it clear you dig him (if you really do that is).

6. Post First Date

An attractive woman is someone who doesn't forget to thank her date for the wonderful company. If you are keen on meeting him again, don't be afraid to mention it. Sometimes, he may want to see you again but a wee bit hesitant to approach you because he may not know what you are thinking. Avoid playing the guessing game, and be honest about your desire to see them again. If you don't wish to see someone again, send them a short message about how nice they are, but it didn't really click for you. End by wishing them well in their quest for finding a date. Forget the three-day cooling off period rule, and call them the next day to find out if they are truly interested in taking it further.

Chapter: Three – Step Three: Talk the Talk

Alright, so maybe by now you've managed to grab their attention or interest. Here comes the tricky part. How do you now sustain their interested and keep them hooked on your conversation skills? Just how do you seduce, attract, and pick-up a man with your words before you get to the real action? Again, you've got help! Here are some proven tips for making stellar conversation with a man to appear more fun, sexy and attractive to him.

What's Your Style?

There's no need to try hard to be something you are clearly not just to please the man. Your cover will be blown sooner or later. Each of us has our own set of strengths, which should be used smartly for keeping a man captivated. What's your style? Are you gregarious and quick-witted? Or more subtle, soft-spoken, and elegant?

Go with your inherent personality and gut feeling while striking a conversation with a man you desire. Keep in mind the setting, situation, and environment. You'll know what works and what doesn't, which will help you to keep improving upon your techniques.

Act Familiar

Even if you haven't interacted with him before, don't appear distant or like strangers. Instead be warm, comfortable and friendly around the object of your desire. Start a casual conversation as if you know each other for long. Men like women who are fun, relaxed and at ease rather than those who are innately conscious about themselves.

Stand in front of the mirror and examine how you look when you talk. Speak in a balanced, even and friendly tone with fairly spaced out speed that you use when talking to your friends. Listen mindfully to how you actually sound and the gestures you make while having a conversation. Try to talk in the same tone and speed when you are around the object of your fancy.

Don't act crazy fascinated or awe-struck by the man. There are few things that put off men as women who go out of the way to please them. They like women who keep their own personality and interests going rather than trying too hard to please. Stay engaging without appearing too eager. There's nothing more charming than a woman who knows how to be her own person. This confidence makes you terribly sexy and desirable and draws him even more to you. When you feel yourself acting like a giddy-headed, love-struck teenager, shift your gaze away from him. Avoid eye contact at such times because you reallydon't want to appear clingy.

Reveal Your Wit and Awesome Sense of Humor

Guys really dig women with a fantastic sense of humor. Find something around you to make a hilarious comment. Stick to light-hearted banter and breezy topics. Don't make a mockery of yourself by playing out the soap opera of your life, much to the amusement of your crush or date. Guys love a playful woman, and quickly bond with women who can keep it fun and humorous.

It takes a huge amount of pressure off the guy's shoulder when you take control of the conversation. He doesn't think the onus of having good time rests upon him alone. This also lightens the mood for him and makes him join in the fun. Of course, not all of us are stand-up comedians reincarnated. Practice using a few funny lines with friends (but please don't make them sound rehearsed) and check their reaction. Be funny by exaggerating things around you or happening in your life.

Appear Open and Interested

Practice active listening while conversing with the man of your dreams. Maintain eye contact, smile flirtatiously and frequently nod to show interest and enthusiasm. Ask interesting questions about what he is saying to show him that you are truly listening to him. Paraphrase the important bits or highlights of his conversation. People totally dig you when they know you care to listen to what they are saying.

Be transparent about your intentions. If you are simply looking for a casual fling or hook-up, let him know that. Similarly, if you are seeking a more long-term and fulfilling relationship, drop hints about that too. Don't appear completely absorbed and besotted by him.

Most importantly, you'll be able to pick up a lot of clues about the type of person he is through his words. It is easy to understand a person's vibe or aura simply by tuning in carefully to what they are saying. Is he the kind who will lead a conversation? Or will he simply sit back and enjoy you taking center stage? Depending on his comfort level, talk or let him do the talking.

Don't behave in an exaggerated manner and laugh at every joke he cracks or gives over the top responses to everything he says in your bid to please him. Space out or even out your reactions a bit, and make them appear more natural and not contrived or forced.

The Ice Breaker

So you see this absolutely drop dead gorgeous guy at the bar, and don't want to wait for him to come and make a conversation. How do you approach the dude? Yes, there are many fabulous pick-up lines that wonder well, but this one seldom fails. Just go near him and tell you, you smell incredibly good. What fragrance are you wearing?

Most men will be glad that you noticed them. Further, complimenting them is like the icing on the cake, they'll be truly flattered. Bonus points, if you can follow it up with something really funny, such as "I went sniffing around here a couple of times because you smelled so good." He'll most likely laugh, and that'll break the ice for further conversation. Who doesn't love a little bit of ego pampering that sounds genuine?

Similarly, if you are both at a party, you can approach him and ask him how he knows the host. You are basically creating a subconscious feeling that there is something in common between the two of you. He'll also know you must be amazing or the common friend wouldn't really be friends with you in the first place. It's like a mutual friends' test. When you see a mutual friend on Facebook, you are likelier to add that person to your friend because in your mind they've already sort of cleared the test by being your friend's friend. It works the same way.

If you are at a restaurant or coffee shop, you may want to compliment him on an accessory (watch never goes wrong, I tell ya) and ask him about it pretending that you've been picked by your office team to buy one as a gift for a co-worker. Watches are to men, what bags and probably stilettos are for a woman. They can never have enough compliments on their watch. You're calling out to their amazing taste in watches, and seeking advice on what you should buy for a co-worker. Bingo! You've hit the jackpot with a bonus of exchanging contact information to get more guidance about purchasing watches. Tralalala!

Trust me when I say this, men are really flattered when you seek their expertise or onion about something. They love to flaunt their knowledge. Even when it comes to something as recommendations from the menu or the type of coffee you should be guzzling, this is one thing that can get them started and going on a positive note. You'll win plenty of brownie points.

At the gym, you may want to ask your potential knight in shining how to use a particular machine or equipment. Men love to show off their expertise and help out whenever needed. This is also the perfect excuse for buying a coffee or protein shake for him to thank him for his training. Take it up from there. Don't forget to make your moves foxier and sexier when he's around, while still focusing on your workout.

If you spot a hottie at a concert, break the ice by asking him how many times he's seen these awesomely talented people performing. If he's totally into them, you'll have a lot in common to talk about. However, even if he hates them and has been dragged to the show, he'll have an interesting backstory to it, which can be a great conversation starter or icebreaker.

Chapter Four – Step Four: Go Flirt Happy Girl

If you're the coy, shy girl type, it may seem like a virtually impossible task to flirt with a man. However, it's much simpler than you actually imagine it to be if you make the right moves. Flirting without actually looking like you're flirting is an art to be mastered. You can rely on an approachable body language, coy gestures, a dazzling smile, light touching, suggestive touching and much more to go flirthappily with the guy of your dreams. There's a lot of flirting you can do via text messages too. Here are some smooth tricks to help you become the ultimate flirt magnet.

Setting the Stage

Girls bear in mind that a guy adores being flirtedwith. Yes, they may not make it obvious or flirt outrageously. But they dig the idea of flirting. It depends on the subtle verbal and non-verbal signals you give them. If your body language is suggestive and seductive, it indicates to them at a subconscious level that you're ready for the flirting game

Let a man know you are warm, friendly and approachable if you want to flirt with him. You are the girl who doesn't really indulging in some well-meaning, flirtatious actions. Men will think a million times before trying to flirt with a woman who appears all prudish and off the limits.

Blush and Be All Coy

Guys love women who are positive, bright and happy. I'll let you in on a secret between you and me – men dig women who smile and laugh a lot while talking to them. Don't appear rude or arrogant when you're with someone you intend to flirt with. Guys run miles away from women who try to be cocky even if they are desirable looking.

Be inviting and warm when talking to your crush. Smile, blush and act coy when he compliments you or says something nice about you. He will do a mini mental dance that his compliment has had the desired effect on you.

Compliment Him Duh

Like I said earlier, guys love to be complimented. It is setting the stage for a flirt happy talk. When you like something about a person, compliment them generously about it. He will adore the fact that you actually noticed a nice thing, and more often than not he'll return the compliment and start having a flirty conversation. When he is being courteous, respectful and chivalrous, thank him for it with an affectionate smile.

When a man's chivalry is appreciated or given a more positive response, he will be even more driven to extend his courtesy and chivalry in your direction. He'll likely be even more warm, open and affectionate.

Drown In His Eyes

One of the biggest secrets of flirting is to do what people generally do when they are head over heels in love with each other. Even though you aren't there already, you don't really have to wait until you get there. Just look excited and happy in his company, and he'll be more than floored.

Next time you talk to a guy you really dig, look straight into his eyes (deeply and intensely) and offer your best smile when he's speaking. It may just end up perplexing him slightly the sight of you staring at him and smiling. However, that'll make him weak in the knees nevertheless. You're connecting at a very sensual level, where you're building a fantastic chemistry.

Tease Your Man

Learn to make fun of the man you fancy in pure jest. Say something like, your joke is lame or try harder Jack. Pulling him down slightly by teasing him in a non-offensive way is a great way to establish friendliness and familiarity. This is something you would do only with close friends or people you are really comfortable with.

By pulling his leg, you are conveying a sense of familiarity. Stay in control of the flirting game by making fun of him and then placing him on a pedestal. I'll let you in on another secret. Men are insanely competitive in nature. When you tease him even playfully, he'll try harder to do something you say he cannot.

Avoid Being Brash, Arrogant and Loud

Every manly guy with a testosterone overdrive loves a feminine or womanly woman or girly girl. Of course, you don't have to be a princess walking in glass slippers. However, do your best to be feminine, soft and subtle in everything from the way you talk to the way you dress. Don't be too brash and loud in a bid to control the conversation. You may not be too happy to read this, but few things piss a guy off as much as rude, arrogant, and loud girls who go around throwing their weight.

Again, you don't have to act all school girl-ish to win the guy's heart. However, you need to (and make that need in caps if you like) make him feel that he can protect you. Through the process of evolution, men have always been hunters, gatherers, and protectors. If you really want to attract a man, you need to give him that feeling every once in a while that he is in control. Let him take the lead sometimes. Play it simple sometimes, hold on and wait for him to take the lead in flirting.

Be Crazy Expressive

I am hoping you've seen at least one episode of Nigella Lawson's show. The gal is well in her middle ages but can give any giddy-headed teenager a run for her money when it comes to making guys go weak in their knees with her flirtatious, expressive and feminine gestures. Be expressive and feminine when you're with the guy you desire.

Spend time in the mirror and work hard on your gestures and expressions. Use your feminine charm to your benefit. I'll bet you when you master this, you'll need no words to have the man on his knees. Practice fluttering your mascara laden eyelids, work hard on getting your smile right and give out tiny little bright expressions. Do this, and you'll be the goddess of all things flirty no man can ever ignore or resist.

Do you think Hollywood actresses and other celebs are born with those insanely killer expressions? It's taken lots of practice to practice those flirtatious moves. Use your feminine expressions to the hilt for completely changing the game when it comes to attracting men like a magnet. Play it up, spice your expressions and just go for the kill lady!

Look Your Best

Flirting with men becomes much easier and way more successful when you look attractive.

Give your persona an added dose of confidence by looking your flattering best. Wear flirty, feminine clothes that highlight your best physical attributes. Opt for shapes and colors that underplay the not so flattering aspects and accentuate your best physical attributes. It's not just about donning micro miniskirts, stilettos and a heavy dose of mascara. The idea is to be well groomed, practice good hygiene and give it your best shot. People are naturally drawn to attractive, confident and presentable women who know how to carry themselves.

Set your hair nicely, keep it clean and fresh smelling. Use a good mouthwash to keep your mouth smelling great. Do your nails. Wear clean, washed and ironed clothes. A nice, well-fitting dress or skirt in red or other bright colors adds to the dazzle and makes you instantly noticeable. Don't be afraid to wear that red lipstick. Sometimes a little make-up can go a long way in playing up your best facial features.

Don't keep the same hairstyle. Try different hairdos such as straight, curly, perm, braid and bun. Experiment with make-up to know what works best for you. Find a look that you truly enjoy putting together and one that gives you confidence. Check out different stores and online catalogs for the season's latest fashion.

Flirt With Touch

Find small excuses to gently touch your crush if you want to flirt with him. It sort of creates a sexual tension and drops a hint about your desire to take it a step ahead.

Gently touch his forearm when you both are talking. When he says something funny, react by reaching your hand out and touching his arm. Put your hand on his shoulder when he is saying something serious just to communicate your support. This is great for creating a mutual camaraderie and reveals that you are completely comfortable around him.

Accidently lean in his direction when you both are walking together. If you are prepared to move to the next level with him, simply brush your hand against his to analyze his reaction.

One sneaky trick that I highly recommend is straightening his collar. Tell him subtly that his collar is slightly crooked and then lean ahead warmly to straighten it for him. Maintain eye contact with him while straightening his collar, and say something like, now that's much better and gently move back. Observe his reaction. I am saying this several times because a man's reaction to your subtle touches will offer you plenty of insights about where you both are headed.

Other signs that you're interested in flirting with him

- Unclenched hands and uncrossed arms and legs.

- Running your fingers subtly through your hair

- Pretend to pick something gently from his jacket

- Face the object of your desire directly while talking

- Wet your lips frequently. Hey and extra points if you bite them discreetly too.

Men are of course able to identify these signs, at least on the subconscious level.

Chapter Five - Step Five: The Seduction Game

It's a well-establishedfact that men are intensely visual creatures. They are majorly controlled by testosterone, which gives you a brilliant opportunity to spice things up. Be the ultimate seduction ninja and temptation goddess by playing out your charm in a way that is impossible for any man to resist. Here are some quick tips that will create a run up to take you both into pleasure zone.

Feel Sexy

How do you plan to seduce the man you desire if you don't feel sexy lady? Want to look and feel sexy without trying? Here's the inside dope on the business of looking good without trying. Join the much sought after sexy club.

Have you ever taken a glance of some random stranger walking on the street and be totally blown away by the sexiness that oozes through them? We all have seen that someone and wondered why the hell hasn't they be signed for any Hollywood flick yet.

Sometimes, you'll notice that they aren't even great looking. So what makes them attractive then? Some of the sexiest folks you'll bump into aren't the prettiest. However, they are still crazy sexy.

What Makes You Sexy

-A fit, healthy and well-built shape/physique

-Good grooming

- Attractive attire

- Sexy inner garments

- Pampering yourself periodically

- Respect yourself and your body

- Enjoy life

- Feel like a sexy goddess

If you fancy being a wild seductress, feel like one. Men are innately visual beings who love boobs and butts, so play it up for them. Perfect moves that accentuate your boobs and butts, and get it right each time. Let him fall for your body. Maintain a posture where your shoulders are pushed back, and your boobs are slightly out. Similarly, walk with your butt slightly out to flaunt it in all its glory. Spice it up by wearing heels, so you get this position naturally, without trying too hard. If you have a pair of toned legs, don't forget to flaunt it.

When you feel like a sexy seductress, it reflects in the way you speak and carry yourself, which in turn attracts a man. Feed into your subconscious mind that you are indeed a sexy siren, who deserves the sexiest men around. This will influence your actions to be more seductive and appealing.

Peek a Boo Baby

Yes, tease him woman! Get his testosterones raging by playing a little peek a boo game. Wear short skirts that reveal a nice pair of thighs or opt for plunging necklines. The sexy outfits will be your highway into a man's heart or ahem anywhere else you want. Of course, you'll need to find a way to ward off all the perverts you'll end up attracting.

If you really want to seduce a man, ensure you don't bear it all and wear tastelessly skimpy clothes. If you show him everything, you aren't leaving anything to his imagination. You aren't effectually challenging his testosterone. It will end up seducing the wrong kind of men or attention. Wear something that offers a teeny-weeny bit of peek a boo without giving it all away.

It is similar to whetting someone's appetite and tempting them for going after the big meal. Offer him a generous peak of what's within too. If he is standing near you, bend down slightly to pick something from the floor or your handbag. A man's eyes dart really fast in the direction of a boob graze. Giving him an exciting preview will make him want to see the entire film.

Don't Throw Yourself at Him

Women, the golden rule for classy seduction is: *Don't ever appear desperate or throw yourself on a man.* Never ever! Again, don't be too obvious in your admiration for him. Play a little hard to get. Appear a little distracted. Find other things to capture your interest. Challenge the man to try harder by appearing distracted. He'll work doubly hard to grab your attention.

If a man gets to know you think he's really hot and into you, he'll not be driven to try hard. For a man, it's all about accomplishments, whether it's a new car, woman or fragrance. It is about acquiring things that aren't easily available or attainable. He's not likely to be enticed or seduced if you make it obvious that you are already into him. That's no fun. He doesn't have to really try hard.

There's no challenge or real achievement is getting something that is easily attainable. That's their logic. He won't be impressed when he realizes you are trying hard to grab his attention. He'll most likely play hard to get (you aren't the only one playing games here lady). For heaven's sake, don't appear trashy, classless and clingy. That's a huge red flag for any man. Turn the table cleverly. Make him chase you by laying an irresistible seduction trail.

Once every while, give him the royal ignore. Stop giving him attention and move to something else when things are going a little too smoothly between you two. Let him not get the feeling that's he's already made a wonderful impression on you. Ruffle up his insecurities by playing slightly hard to get.

Hit the Dance Floor

There's nothing more seductive than showing your crush all the right moves on a dance floor. You can move your body in a certain way to floor him right out there on the dance floor. If you can pick one place to go with a man you intend to seduce, opt to go clubbing.

Move your way around his body seductively while dancing together. Lean against him, show off your foxy moves and build sexual chemistry that's just waiting to explode later. Leave him something to think about with touches that linger.

Purposefully Stage Awkward Situations

Yes, you want the guy's heart and trousers to be full, don't you? Wink wink! The smart girl's guide to seducing a man comprises purposely creating awkward situations where you both are left in close physical proximity to each other.

Squeeze into a packed elevator with him, of course 'unknowingly.' Allow your butt to slightlybrush against his leg. If he's seated, just turn up from behind him and reach out for something that he placed on his table. Do this when he isn't looking. When the guy turns slightly to look at you, he will brush against your breasts. Tada! The trick is to rub your feminine parts against him. Don't make the moves obvious or if he gets everything on a platter, he won't really appreciate it much.

Even when you hug him to greet him, ensure your girly parts rub against him.If you don't make it obvious, he'll realize he is lucky to be able to touch you in seemingly off the limit places. Create situations where he gets an opportunity to touch you. The idea is to get his pants a wee bit tighter, so he fantasizes all the more about you.

Don't Underestimate the Power of Good Fragrance

One of the most overpowering subconscious influences that trigger a man's judgment is scent. A survey revealed that a staggering 89 percent men believe that a powerful scent boosts the attractiveness of a lady. And, hold it. About 55 percent of those men went ahead and stated they would get amorous only because they find a woman's perfume appealing.

Scent is often the most potent subconscious influencers when it comes to affecting our decision or feelings about the opposite sex. This is actually comparable at a very primordial level to the pheromones used by animals during the mating game.

Pro tip- As a woman, you can multiply your pheromone levels by using natural oils such as rose, jasmine, and ylang-ylang, which are famous for their aphrodisiac features. The guy will go into a tizzy simply by your presence.

Remember how Cleopatra welcomed Marc Anthony on a ship with scented sails? The exotic fragrance drove him to fall head over heels in love with her, so much so, he died for her. Moral of the story, use a sexy, subtle and feminine scent to seduce your man. However, ensure you don't go overboard because you don't really want to send the man on an allergic coughing fit, do you? Opt for floral, citrusy and light blends.

Apply it on the body's pulse points, on your wrists, behind the ears, on the elbow bend, right behind your knees and on the ankle's insides. Again, a little tip to make your aura even more fragrant and mysterious. Release a little perfume right in the air, while walking into it.

Make the smell synonymous with you, so the guy finds it really difficult to forget you. Our olfactory glands are closely connected with neurons associated with memory and retention, which is why certain smells instantly trigger specific memories for us. When a man can clearly associate a smell with you, he will find it virtually impossible to forget you. Let your fragrance be deeply embedded in the man's mind.

Use Messaging and Snapchat Ladies

There's no reason why you cannot seduce a man who isn't around. Plus, you'll be less intimated and bolder when you aren't doing it face to face. Send the guy sexy or proactive messages, pictures, or snapchats. Don't send overtly revealing pictures or again, you aren't leaving much for his imagination.

Let the dude know you dig him by transferring a picture of something subtle, classy and fun that doesn't border on obscene. How about you frolicking in a pool to spark his raging imagination? Get him thinking in the right direction.

Send him dirty messages that leave things to his imagination and compel him to think. For example, "I had this mad dream about you last time" or "I just saw something that reminded me of you." Always works!

How about something seemingly innocuous that's loaded with innuendos such as "I intend to blow your mind completely" Now it can imply a lot of things including a blowjob or that you are going to show him something really amazing. It creates an irresistible anticipation that is hard to match.

You'll notice that these messages aren't really sexual in nature. The objective is to get him wondering and pumping up the excitement. You are basically telling him exactly what may be music to his ears. Pro tip – send him a message that is short and snappy, and doesn't demand a reply.

Try to test his reaction by sending a few messages. If things don't go as expected, you can always cover it up "Oh! My apologies that message was meant for someone else." He'll be all the more subconsciously enraged as to why you meant it to someone else. Remember, stimulating a man's competitive streak always works wonders?

You'll wriggle your way out of an awkward situation, while stilling awakening his competitive spirit. Don't freak him out be sending really obvious and in your face messages that border more on sleaziness. Men abhor an overt display of crassness and sleaziness by a woman. They like it when you keep it fun, flirty, naughty and suggestive, but definitely not tasteless. You'll end up attracting the wrong kind of men if they are impressed with your sleaziness.

Chapter Six – Step Six: How to Get Him Crazy in Bed

Congratulations, you've finally gotten the object of your desire into bed with owing to your hard to resist charm. You diva you! Now it's time to steam things up in the bed in such a way that he just cannot resist your charms and get enough of you. There's a lot you can do by using some imagination and inspired moves.

It is time to replace ho-hum vanilla sex with steamier, spicier and more incredible acts. How about toys, flavored lubricants, and playful lingerie? Think an array of costumes and role play. Here are some ways to make the action under the sheets even more exciting.

1. Get giddier and frisker by popping a bottle of champagne in bed. You'll go back to being tipsy, don't care a damn about the world teens.

2. Light up a few fragrant candles in the background, and play soft music. The ambiance should reflect your soft and seductive mood.

3. Slow things down rather than rushing into rabid, zealous sex as soon as you hit the bed. Do things that prolong your time in the

bedroom. Build tension in a manner that it leads to exploding pleasure.

4. Leaving love notes like a little bedroom treasure hunt game, where you send him chasing different clues until he discovers something that you are going to do with him that will completely blow his mind away.

5. Massages are a great run up to the actual sexual activity. Offer him gentle messages near his erogenous zones to get him wet and hard. It builds anticipation for the slowly commencing sexual activity. Ask the man to on his stomach. Apply gentle thumb pressure on his lower back. Move upwards gradually and sensually. You'll barely be able to reach his shoulders before he gets all fired up for action.

6. Set a few rules to build a high sense of anticipation. For example, you may want to spend some days necking and making out with your clothes still on. The next few days can be spent touching each other everywhere except genitals. Then, use your mouth instead of hands for giving pleasure. By the end of these few days, he'll be left with a huge arousal overflow that will be waiting to explore. It will lead to heavy-duty craving in his erogenous and pleasure zones.

7. Ditch predictability and savor an amazing sex life. Go down the unpredictable route by changing the location a bit. You don't need

to be in the bedroom to make humdrum love. Get steaming on a pool table in the house or even a garage. When there are people around the two of you, lock your eyes to make love. Cast a few suggestive glances in your man's direction. Enjoy a round of foreplay and sex in the open. Making love under the open sky and reaching orgasm heaven gives him an altogether different high.

8. Keep all gadgets away from the bedroom. When you're enjoying the action in the bed, it's just the two of you. There should be nothing in between, including smartphones, blaring television sets and electronic gadgets. Focus on building the atmosphere of pleasure, excitement, and intimacy.

9. Play fantasy bowl for a nice lead-up to frenzied action later. Write your three most intense and deepest sexual fantasies that no one knows about. Get your man to follow suit by mentioning three of his most intense sexual fantasies. Collect the chits and throw it in a bowl. Shuffle the chits and pick up chits by turn. Talk explicitly about the fantasy that comes up. Both swap notes about how they want the act fulfilled. There's no sexual activity yet. You are simply talking about the fantasy. Now turn off the lights and get under the sheets. Allow him to describe his fantasy while you throw your hands below the sheet. You both will be monstrously aroused before your guy finishes talking.

10. Play sex dice the next time you want to steam it up in the bedroom. All that is needed is a pair of fun adult dice that can be sourced from an adult store. Make two categories of love notes. On

one set, mention sensual body parts and on another, various actions that you'd like on those body parts. It can create an amazing array of exciting combinations when you pick one of each category. Keep it fresh, try totally different positions, and work on your intimacy.

Men adore women who take the lead, are unafraid to try new things and open to a variety of experiences. They love an adventurous, exciting and proactive gal. So, don't hesitate to climb over him and get going! That's a huge-huge turn on for your man.

11. How about giving him some much needed wet pleasures? Men love action under the shower. Start by kissing each other passionately under the shower. Work up a rich lather to wash each other sensuously. It will not just leave you both smelling fresh, but also build plenty of sexual tension for the actual act to follow. How about some passionate necking and kissing on the couch or in the dark, last row of a less crowded cinema?

12. A dirty dancing or stripping session can be the perfect prelude to several passionate, raunchy and foxy moves to follow.

13. Tie him up to the best with a pair of your sexiest stockings or leggings. Move your mouth/tongue over his erogenous zones. Place a high pillow under his head so he can clearly see all your moves and get sufficiently wet or aroused. Tease by going down on him and moving back until he cannot take it anymore.

14. Whisper sweet nothings in his ear. Few things stimulate a man's sexual drive as much as cooing softly his ears. Tell him everything you intend to do to him during your time in bed. Follow this up by kissing him lightly on the lower neck.

15. Walk around the house wearing racy underwear and a sexy pair of stilettos. This is another little gem that works like magic. The man will not want anything else but to see you strut around making sexy moves that are bound to send his testosterones gushing.

Chapter Seven – Step Seven: Keep Your Man Hooked and Happy

Now that you've got him, how do you keep him happily hooked and addicted to you? It takes more than just romantic and gestures to have him eating out of your hands and obeying everything you say. Here are some of the most powerful tips to have a man completely wrapped around your little finger.

1. Praise him publically. Few things are more effective when it comes to boosting your guy's ego than appreciating him openly in front of people. He'll feel a huge surge of gratitude and affection for you. Men love women who stand by then, believe in their abilities and support them. Do this, and he'll melt faster than wax.

2. Keep him feeling secure. Men have oversized egos, there's no denying this. The flipside, their egos are also extremely fragile. They are territorial by nature and feel easily threatened. Keep them secure in the right manner, and they'll adore you for it. Let him know that you are his if you are truly a committed and mutually exclusive couple.

3. Surprise him once in a while. Really now, it isn't solely a man's domain to buy you expensive gifts, chocolates, and flowers. Of course, you love to be pampered but so does he. Buy him

something that he has been eyeing for long but hasn't got around to buy. These little surprise gifts will speak volumes about your thoughtfulness and affection for him. It'll also convey to him that you aren't simply a gold digging receiver by also someone who cares to give. Make him feel like he is indeed the luckiest man on earth to have someone like you in his life.

4. Don't let go of your inner child. Seriously, as much as men prefer a matured and in control woman, they always love someone who is a free spirit and hasn't lost touch with her inner child. A woman who is spontaneous, fun and radiates a childlike enthusiasm is fun and easy to be. She takes the stress and burdens off a man's shoulder. This is exactly why a wise person once said, "be a girl at heart and a woman in spirit." Most women mother their men and get annoyed the man behaves childishly.

Instead of behaving like a nag, simply join in the fun once in a while and act like crazy kids. He'll love that you are not playing his mother or class monitor all the time. Let him be comfortable revealing his child side in front of you. He'll love you for it.

5. Food is the fastest route to man's heart, yes! On the face of it, they'll say your cooking skills don't really matter to them. Give him a gastronomy orgasm every once in a while by whipping up his favorite meal. He'll be hopelessly hooked. Make a reservation at his favorite restaurant when you know he's busy with work and hasn't had the opportunity to dine there for long. Invest time and effort on special occasions to come up with a delicious, home-

made meal. He'll appreciate the thoughtfulness and effort behind the act.

6. Seek his expert counsel, emotional support or help. A man loves to be your knight in shining armor. He wants to know that he is useful and valuable in your life. When you seek his help and counsel every now and then, his position as a problem solves is reinforced. He feels a sense of delight in making life easy for you. When you are feeling low, drained and helpless, simply walk into his arms for him to comfort you. He will be overwhelmed by the fact that he is making you feel slightly better in the middle of all that stress.

7. Avoid emasculating him. Don't belittle him or make him feel less of a man when he's made a mistake, especially in public. It doesn't help to show him down. Men don't like to be told they are wrong straight off. If he feels less of a man with your constant putting down, he will most likely seek that validation and feeling of manliness from elsewhere.

8. Don't stop dating him or flirting with him. Just because you are a couple now doesn't mean you stop doing all the fun things. Keep the passion in your relationship alive by trying fun, new things together. Plan creative dates, don't hesitate to try novel adventures/activities together and go discover different places. Pinch his butt for naughty fun or brush your hand against his thigh playfully. Don't forget to indulge in a wee bit of sexting throughout the day.

9. Be open. Thisapplies to plenty of things that you would together, including trying a new eatery in town or a new move in the bedroom. Each person has varied tastes, and to keep it interesting and exciting, you've got to keep a flexible and non-judgmental mind. As long as something doesn't hurt or is against your morals/ethics, give it a go if he likes it. Even if you want to refuse something, do it politely and diplomatically without offending him.

10. Avoid using sex as an exchange chip. Don't withhold sex because he didn't do the dishes or refused to go out with your friends. Making it a bartering chip takes its toll on the act, and ultimately your relationship. He will most likely believe that sex is just another chore or weapon rather than a pleasurable activity for you. Eventually, constant bartering will take a toll on your man, and he'll be looking for pleasure elsewhere.

11. Avoid saying unflattering things behind his back. All couples have their share of conflicts and challenges. Unless he is doing something that is unlawful or being physically/mentally abusive (in these cases you should surely seek counseling and legal help), spare your relationship the drama by involving other people in it. Don't go on a ranting spree with your family and friends. Discussing your couple problems with others can often make it worse.

12. Make your man a priority. Take the time and effort to let him know he's craved for and special even after you get him. Don't just

snag him as just another acquisition and take him for granted once he is yours. Despite a busy schedule and other commitments, ensure you make time for him. It can be anything from booking tickets to watch his favorite game to sending him an affectionate text message during the day to picking up a snack he loves on the way from work. Its small gestures like these that reveal you really care. He'll know he's always on the top of your mind with these thoughtful acts.

13. Don't be an attention seeking diva. Men don't fancy drama queens and attention seeking divas. Sooner or later, they'll get tired of your shenanigans and dump you for someone who is calm, comfortable and in control. Yes, wanting his attention is alright but going to the extreme end of the spectrum regularly to be a whine queen is a different game altogether. Attention-grabbing tactics are not seductive; they are annoying, stressful and desperate. Don't seek constant validation and attention from others. Forcing attention to yourself is a huge off, and make you unattractive to him.

14. Avoid being a nag. Don't create catastrophic metaphors out of unwashed dishes and wet towels on the bed. Women unknowingly annoy their partners by making a huge deal of trivial daily habits. Tone down the nag factor and overlook these things sometimes. Women often blow things up and start equating a man's habits as a measure of their love. For instance, He didn't pick up the crumbs from the table after I told him, which means he really doesn't love me. Remind him in a more gentle, affectionate, and humorous way

when approaching your man for doing something or changing a habit.

Conclusion

Thank you for purchasing the book, "*How to Attract Men: The Right Way*".

I sincerely hope you enjoyed reading it. I also hope the book was able to offer you a ton of actionable, practical, and easily applicable techniques to not just attract men but also keep them completely addicted to you.

The next step is to take action. Apply all these little-known secret strategies and wisdom nuggets to become the ultimate diva or man-guy magnet. Use all these killer secrets and psychological tricks to unlock the male mind to literally have him wrapped around your little finger.

Irrespective of where you are in the dating game currently, start applying these methods to experience a complete transformation from a socially awkward gal to one who gets the male species weak in their knees. It takes some practice and consistent efforts of course, but it's worth it to be a diva.

Here's to being a confident, desirable, interesting and fun guy magnet!

HOW TO
FLIRT
THE RIGHT WAY
The Only 7 Steps You Need to Master Flirting, Seduction and Sexual Tension Whilst Dating Today
DEAN MACK

BOOK 2: HOW TO FLIRT

THE RIGHT WAY

The Only 7 Steps You Need to Master Flirting, Seduction and Sexual Tension Whilst Dating Today

Dean Mack

This document is geared towards providing exact and reliable information in regards to the topic and issue covered. The publication is sold with the idea that the publisher is not required to render accounting, officially permitted, or otherwise, qualified services. If advice is necessary, legal or professional, a practiced individual in the profession should be ordered.

From a Declaration of Principles which was accepted and approved equally by a Committee of the American Bar Association and a Committee of Publishers and Associations.

The information provided herein is stated to be truthful and consistent, in that any liability, in terms of inattention or otherwise, by any usage or abuse of any policies, processes, or directions contained within is the solitary and utter responsibility of the recipient reader. Under no circumstances will any legal responsibility or blame be held against the publisher for any reparation, damages, or monetary loss due to the information herein, either directly or indirectly.

Table of Contents

Introduction

This book is designed to help you master the art of flirting in seven simple steps. When you master the art of flirting, you make it so that you can effortlessly flirt with anyone you are attracted to. Not only does it make flirting itself easier, but it also builds your self-confidence, increases your charisma, and makes otherwise vulnerable romantic encounters much easier to navigate.

As a result of practicing the seven skills that you will learn within this book, you will be able to have great success with flirting with the people that you are attracted to. Not only will you be able to effortlessly gain their attraction, but you will also be able to keep your encounters positive and enjoyable. You will learn exactly how you can earn their attraction *and* keep it simply by employing these seven steps and using them over and over again.

If you are ready to stop feeling so uncomfortable in flirtatious encounters, you have come to the right place. This book will ensure that all uncertainty is erased and that you are the leader in the conversation. Not only will your naturally-boosted self-confidence further increase your romantic interest's attraction toward you, but it will also help move you through these seven steps effortlessly! If you follow them carefully and build on them, you will find that flirting is effortless. Now, if you are ready to get started, please do so. And, of course, enjoy!

Chapter 1: Don't Overthink It

One of the biggest ways that we make flirting with others hard is by overthinking it. Often when we develop an attraction for someone, especially someone we've known for some time, it can be hard not to overthink the situation. You may find yourself constantly dreaming of what it would be like to have a successful flirtatious conversation with them and attract them into wanting to be with you. Because you dream and think of it so much, you end up putting the entire possibility on a pedestal. This means that you mentally create the illusion that it is much harder for you to attain than it actually is. The result of overthinking is that you are so psyched out that you struggle to successfully flirt at all. Instead, you might find yourself intimidated by the idea and struggling to even form coherent sentences that create a decent conversation. So, the first step to be successful with flirting is to refrain from overthinking it.

Before you begin learning how you can refrain from overthinking it, let's take a look at what overthinking it looks like in real life:

You work in an office building. Your office is down the hall from the person whom you are presently attracted to. Each day you pass each other to get to your respective offices. At first, you felt it was easy to say hello and ask them how their morning was going. You noticed they were good looking but hadn't yet developed a full attraction for them. After a few weeks, you notice their smile. You can't seem to get their smile out of your head. You also start noticing other things you like about them, such as how charismatic they are, and how they are always thinking about others. Before long you are full on attracted to this person. Now, it seems like you are constantly thinking about all of the ways you like them. When you see them walk past your office you dream that they poke their head inside and you two flirt effortlessly. The longer this state of attraction goes on, the harder it seems to be for you to talk to this person. You have put so much pressure on what you want from the relationship before ever taking action that now, suddenly, you find that you are intimidated by this person. It has become harder for you to say hello in the morning without feeling uncomfortable, and the small talk you used to share in the lunchroom seems to have gone away because you find that you're too nervous to keep it going. You have spent too much time overthinking and not enough time actually acting on the attractions you are feeling.

As you can see, overthinking your attraction to someone else increases the intimidation that you feel from the idea of flirting with them. You may have success flirting on small scales, but the idea of taking it anywhere beyond flirting might be enough to make you feel extremely uncomfortable.

The problem with overthinking is that we often end up setting enormous expectations on how our interactions will go. Then, because it is unlikely that these expectations will actually be met by the other person, it becomes harder to talk to them. Not only are we intimidated by what we have made them to be in our head, but we are also fearful of the idea of feeling rejected by them. For example, maybe you imagined that the first time you flirted with someone you were attracted to that they would give you their phone number or ask you out on a date. If this doesn't happen, you end the conversation feeling extremely rejected and unhappy with the interaction because your expectations were not met.

When you don't invest time in overthinking, you don't have the opportunity to create expectations of who you think that person truly is and what your shared interactions will be like. Instead, you have the opportunity to stay light and attentive and enjoy any outcome from the conversation. You can invest yourself in the conversation and if you get a positive result, such as a phone number, you can feel successful in your interaction. If you have the conversation and it doesn't go well, however, you can leave with a smile. Because you had no expectations, it is easier for you to move on. As well, you can learn from the interaction so that you can experience greater success with your flirting attempts in the future.

Here is an example of how the above situation might turn out if you were to stop overthinking it and simply act on how you feel:

You work in an office building. Your office is down the hall from the person whom you are presently attracted to. At first you only said hello to each other each morning, but over time the conversation grew. You started lightly flirting with the person and were pleasantly surprised when they returned the attention. As the days went by, your flirting became more recognizable. By now you were both clearly attracted to each other as the flirting had gone past playful friendliness. One day in the lunchroom while you were flirting with the person you liked they asked for your number. Your relationship continued to grow through text messages and the occasional phone call until eventually they asked you on a date.

Because you weren't overthinking the experience in this situation, you were able to stop setting expectations and worrying that they wouldn't be met. As a result, you were able to allow the flirting to start organically and the relationship to grow naturally over time. In the end you got exactly what you wanted, which was a date with the person you were attracted to. Instead of overthinking the outcome you simply let it come naturally and were pleasantly surprised when it worked out in your favor.

Overthinking is something we all tend to do. We don't only do it around flirting, either. In fact, we tend to overthink about many things in our lives! We often overthink about important meetings and interviews, interactions we will share with other people, situations we may find ourselves in, and more! All of this overthinking tends to reinforce this behavior in each area of our life, meaning we are much more likely to overthink about flirting if we are already actively overthinking about other things in our lives as well. The best way to prevent yourself from overthinking is to learn how to reduce overthinking altogether. The following tips will help you achieve just that:

Notice When You're Stuck in Your Head

When people are used to overthinking they often fail to recognize when it is actually happening. The first step to overcoming overthinking is to take the time to practice becoming self-aware of this habit and notice when you're doing it. When you are aware of the problem and you can easily identify when it is happening it becomes much easier to resolve it and prevent yourself from overthinking in the future. The best way to tell if you are overthinking something is if you notice that you are replaying events in your head over and over or if you can't seem to stop obsessing over a particular topic. If your thoughts aren't focused on a resolution or something positive, you are likely overthinking about the very topic at hand. This is when you can start executing the steps to overcome overthinking.

Focus on Problem-Solving

Dwelling on problems occurs when we find ourselves obsessing over the problem itself instead of focusing on potential solutions that could assist us in resolving the problem. If you find that you are paying attention to problems, start looking for solutions. Keeping your focus on problem-solving instead of problems themselves is a great way to ensure that you are no longer overthinking the problem. It is important to pay attention to this step as many people make one simple mistake: they find a solution to a problem but then immediately begin to find problems in the solution. Once you have chosen a solution, or a couple if it is a larger situation with many possible outcomes, make an agreement with yourself that you will then let the information subside from your mind. Take decisive action based on the solutions you have chosen and then make a pact with yourself that you will not pay attention to any further problems *unless* one actually arises after you have taken action. Don't imagine problems that aren't real as this is a sneaky form of overthinking that can keep you trapped in the cycle!

Challenge Your Thoughts

Many times we get carried away with negative thoughts because we have given ourselves the ability to believe that they are genuinely real and are likely going to happen. For example, we may overthink flirting with someone because we are afraid they are going to reject us and we will be left feeling badly about ourselves. It is important to remember that fear and other emotions can cause us to look at situations too intimately and stop us from stepping back and looking at them rationally. If you find yourself obsessing over a particular thought, challenge it. Challenge the topic by putting it under a microscope for a minute. Ask questions such as: "What is the likelihood that this outcome could actually happen?" And, "If it did happen, how bad would it actually be?" If you answer these questions honestly without emotional attachment to the answers, in many cases you will likely find that you are far too worried about something that is unlikely to happen.

Practice Reflection

Although this is not necessarily a tip to help with overcoming overthinking about flirting specifically, reflection is a good way to prevent ourselves from overthinking in general which can reduce our likelihood to overthink about flirting. Reflection means that you give yourself the opportunity to genuinely look back on problems you are facing and take the time to look them over. Reflect on what they are, how they make you feel, and the likelihood of you being able to overcome the problem. If you can, look for solutions during this time, too. We tend to obsess over problems when we don't give ourselves adequate time to reflect on them and invest quality time in our thoughts so that we can work through them and then release them. In other words, because you are trying so hard to put it out of your mind you are not giving the problem the attention it needs and so it is making you worry more. A great way to overcome this habit is to stop yourself from obsessing by intentionally spending time reflecting on any problems you are experiencing. Setting aside "thinking time" on a daily basis is an excellent way to ensure that you are getting enough time to reflect on your problems, discover solutions, and allow yourself to move on from the thought.

Learn to Be Mindful

Mindfulness is a great skill you can use to help build self-awareness and mental strength. When you are mindful, you increase your ability to not only identify overthinking patterns but also intentionally overcome them. Mindfulness takes you out of the constant state of worrying and places you back into the present where you can focus on what you are currently experiencing, rather than what you have concocted in your mind. Some great practices you can use to build mindfulness skills include: meditation, visualization, concentration-building practices, and more. If you want to focus on building mindfulness specifically, there are many free courses, guides, videos, and other resources you can use to help you with this skill.

Change the Tune of Your Thoughts

Sometimes, stopping ourselves from overthinking can be as easy as mentally "changing the channel" on your thoughts. Simply telling yourself to stop thinking about something may result in you thinking about it more because you have put even more attention on the subject. Instead, completely change the tune of your thoughts by choosing a new thought entirely. If you are obsessing over the idea of flirting with someone you like, for example, you might instead change your thoughts to work you need to complete or what you are going to each for lunch when your break time comes. By completely changing the course of your thoughts altogether you don't only ask your mind to stop thinking about something you no longer want to dwell on, but you also give it something new to think about. This form of distraction is a great way to quickly overcome overthinking by intentionally placing your thoughts elsewhere.

Chapter 2: Make Use of Eye Contact

Eye contact has a powerful impact on how we connect with other people. In many cases, we make eye contact before we even start verbally communicating with someone else. It is a powerful way to start a connection with someone else and to deepen that connection. Eye contact instantly makes people more interested in you as it makes them feel like you are intentionally trying to draw their attention in.

Let's take a look at what might happen if you avoid using eye contact:

You are out with your friends at a bar. As your friend goes to order more drinks, you notice someone attractive standing at the other end of the bar. When they look up at you, you quickly dodge your eyes away and look elsewhere. You look back a few moments later to notice that the person is now talking to and flirting with someone else.

Since you dodged eye contact, the person you were attracted to talked to someone else. It is likely that the person they did end up talking to made eye contact before approaching them, or being approached by them, for the conversation to start. When you avoid eye contact with someone you subliminally send them a signal that you are not open for communication. They are quickly turned off and will look elsewhere for someone else to communicate with.

Let's take a look at what might have happened if you used eye contact instead:

You are out with your friends at a bar. As your friend goes to order more drinks, you notice someone attractive standing at the other end of the bar. Suddenly, they look up and you make eye contact. You hold it for a moment before breaking the eye contact to see how your friend is progressing with your drink order. When you look back, you notice that person looks back as well. You hold eye contact a bit longer this time and smile at them. They smile back and then head your way to strike up a conversation. Or, they smile back but are too shy to walk up to you. Instead, you walk over to them and begin talking.

Since you both made the effort to make use of eye contact it became increasingly clear to both of you that you were interested in a conversation. You both gave the subliminal signal that said you were "open for communication" and so you acted on it. Now, you are able to chat and use other flirting techniques to keep them interested and create a successful flirtatious interaction.

Eye contact, although important, is not something we think of often. It is important to make eye contact when you want to begin communicating with someone, and it is also important to keep eye contact during the conversation. While you don't need to stare into their eyes constantly, you should be looking into their eyes more often than not. This helps the person feel like you are communicating directly with them, as though they have your full attention. When we are flirting, it is important that we are very intentional about our focus and that the person we are flirting with knows that they are the center of our focus at the time.

People who struggle to create or maintain eye contact struggle to flirt and create successful connections with other people because they struggle to convey what they actually mean and feel. When you don't make eye contact you tend to come off as nervous, under confident, uninterested, or otherwise not approachable for the person you are communicating with, even if this is not true.

Some great ways to improve your ability to maintain eye contact include:

- Overcome nervousness. Refrain from overthinking, which tends to be one of the primary causes of nervousness, and instead allow yourself to simply "be" in the moment.
- Avoid "eye crutches". These are anything we may focus on instead of the person we are talking to, often giving the impression that we are interested in something

other than the person we are actively communicating with.

- Practice. Instead of expecting yourself to do great right away, especially in difficult or vulnerable situations, look for opportunities to practice eye contact throughout the day. Use it when you are talking to cashiers or baristas, when you are communicating with friends and family, and even when you are talking with coworkers. The more you practice using eye contact in your regular daily conversations, the more natural it will feel for you.
- Spend time listening to others. One major skill in active listening involves you maintaining eye contact with the person you are communicating with. Since listening *and* eye contact are both great ways to improve your ability to flirt with others, investing in this particular skill can help you have greater success when it comes to flirting.
- Look at the color of their eyes. One way many people improve their eye contact is to look at the color of people's eyes. Look for unique traits that they may have and pay attention as deeply as you can to these qualities. When you are looking this intently it not only helps you maintain your eye contact, but it also helps you have good quality eye contact.

- Pretend the person you are talking to is the only thing in the room. When you eliminate any distractions that may take your attention away it becomes a lot easier to focus on the person you are talking to, especially by maintaining eye contact.
- Practice mindfulness. Once again, improving your mindfulness abilities is a great way to increase your ability to maintain eye contact with people. When you are able to intentionally maintain your focus on something without your attention constantly turning elsewhere, it becomes much easier for you to maintain eye contact. You will no longer struggle with the feeling that you need to constantly look for distractions or find other ways to keep yourself interested because you will be able to intentionally and actively remain interested in the person you are talking to.

A great exercise to help you improve your ability to maintain eye contact is to give yourself opportunities to practice. Try scanning a room the next time you're in a place that has many people, such as a restaurant. When you find someone willing to reciprocate, hold eye contact for a few seconds before breaking it to pay attention elsewhere. Then, a few moments later, look back in the direction of that person. When you catch their eye contact, hold it again a bit longer. This time, smile when you do. You want to practice holding their eye contact for at least two seconds before you look away again.

If the idea of looking away and looking back seems too difficult or intimidating in the beginning, try simply holding eye contact for at least two seconds and smiling the first time around. When you have grown comfortable using this strategy, then try increasing it to the two looks.

Practicing this strategy will not only increase your confidence in capturing and maintaining eye contact, but it will also help the skill feel more natural to you. Furthermore, as you practice you are likely to open yourself up to conversations with people. This means that while you are practicing eye contact itself, you may even land yourself the opportunity to practice flirting with someone who was attracted to you from this little trick!

Chapter 3: Light Touching

The power of effective touch is incredible. When you subtly touch someone else you show them that you are interested in them, but you also increase the physical attraction between the two of you. This is a tried and true flirting method that is known to help give a clear signal that you are attracted to the person in front of you and to help open their attraction toward you as well.

There are many things to pay attention to when you are practicing lightly touching the person you are flirting with. Because you *are* physically touching the other person, you must always ensure that you are respecting boundaries and are not touching them in an unwanted or inappropriate way. Using touch in the wrong way can result in you turning the other person off and may close the door on your ability to flirt with them in the future. It is important that when you practice lightly touching other people that you are respectful of their boundaries and that the touch is gentle and friendly, not uncomfortable and unwanted.

Aside from ensuring that you are being mindful of people's personal space and are not interfering with their comfort in a negative way, there are some other things you should know about light touching when you are flirting. First, you should know why this technique works!

When you lightly touch someone as you are flirting with them, it physically closes the space between you. This gives the subliminal message that you want to be closer with that person. Since we rarely want to be physically closer to people that we are only friendly with, this gives them a subtle signal that you are genuinely interested in them and that you want to be closer with them. Lightly touching their hand, arm, shoulder, upper back, or even their knee if you are sitting down are all great ways to use light touch during the process of flirting. You always want to make sure, however, that the moment is fleeting and that you are gentle about it. Being too playful about this practice may turn it into a playful touch instead of a flirtatious touch. If this happens, you might find that you completely change the message behind the act itself.

In addition to closing the gap between you and the person you are flirting with, touch is also known to help release chemicals that make you feel good. Studies have shown that touching another individual releases a chemical in both of you known as oxytocin. This chemical is responsible for creating loving sensations within your body. To many, it is known as the “love hormone” or the “cuddle hormone” because it gives you the urge to want to be closer to the person you have touched or been touched by.

The key to using touch as a form of flirting is to start using this technique early on in the process and use it often. You want to start with very light and brief touching. For example, laughing at their joke and gently touching the other person’s arm while you lean in toward them slightly. Make sure the earlier touches are brief and extremely light. Since this person is not yet used to the touching sensation coming from you, you want to be very gentle and easy about it to avoid creating any feelings of discomfort or displeasure.

Aside from keeping it light and appropriate, there are very few things you should worry about when it comes to using touch as a form of flirting. Of course, the more you do it the better results you will have. Don't make it feel forced, however. You want to ensure that you are doing it in an organic way that feels natural to the conversation, not like you are being touchy or pushy. Furthermore, if it seems like the person does not enjoy it and they are not reciprocating your emotions or attraction, refrain from further touching. Stay mindful to the present situation that you are in and allow it to flow naturally. Being too pushy or touching when touches are unwanted, such as if the person is not reciprocating your attraction, can actually turn the person off further. Take it slow and easy and pay attention to the signs you are getting from the other person.

If you are unsure about how you can naturally incorporate touch into your flirting, try these to get started:

- When you see the person after not seeing them for a while, place your hand gently on their shoulder and make eye contact when asking how they're doing. If you haven't been flirting long, remove your hand after a few seconds. If you have, let it linger. If you have been flirting for a while, move in for a hug after they have answered you.

- Give the person you are flirting with a genuine compliment while lightly placing your hand on their hand or arm. For example, say: "Oh my gosh, your eyes are beautiful!" while gently touching their hand from across the table.
- If you feel your legs touch when you sit next to each other, let them stay that way. Don't pull back from the touch.

In addition to touch, there are many other forms of body language you can use when you are flirting. Although these forms don't necessarily involve you touching the other person, they do help give a physical signal that you are interested in them. Body language accounts for a large portion of our ability to communicate with each other, so incorporating it as a part of your communication strategies is a great way to maximize your success with flirting, seducing, and dating other people. The following list will give you some great ideas of types of body language you can use when you are flirting with people.

Show Off

Despite the fact that we are humans, we still have an animalistic tendency to "show off" to the people we are attracted to. While there have been significant studies done around this subject to explain why, we are primarily going to focus on how. The best way to show off is to accentuate your features.

If you are a female, sit in a way that allows the person you are attempting to attract the opportunity to get an ample view of your cleavage. Face the person you are flirting with and draw attention to your curves, your eyes, your lips, and anywhere else on your body that may be seductive.

For men, you typically want to show off your strength. Keep your arms, especially your biceps, visible and make subtle efforts to show them off to her. You can also keep your shoulders broad and show off other strong features you have. As well, draw attention into your eyes and mouth.

For both genders, you want to sit tall and confidence. Straighten your back, keep your shoulders level, and keep your chin up with your face attentive. Face the person you are talking to so they can see as much of you as possible, but also to show that you are paying attention to them and that your full focus is on them. Keep your posture natural but strong to show off how confident you are.

Mirror Their Motions

One big way that you can flirt with someone through body language is to mirror the motions they make. If they touch their hair, for example, you can touch yours. You may notice that you do this automatically without actually thinking about it. This is because this is a natural form of body language that we use to attract other people and show our interest in them.

When you are intentionally mirroring someone's motions, ensure that you are not overdoing it. Don't touch everywhere on your body that they touch. Instead, mirror there motions every few moments to get the best results. When you do, be subtle about it. Glance at what they're doing, do it yourself in your own unique way, catch their eye contact once again and smile. Make it seem like it was a coincidence that you both felt the urge to do it at the same time, rather than you intentionally trying to copy what they are doing.

Additionally, you can gauge someone's interest in you by watching for the same mirroring act. If they touch their hair a few moments after you've touched yours, or you notice that they are otherwise mirroring you, even if it is unintentionally, then you know that they are attracted to you.

Use Facial Expressions

One of the biggest ways we communicate through body language is through facial expressions. Use your facial expressions to your advantage so that the person you are flirting with can read you like a book. For example, if they are telling you about themselves, look at them intently, but also seductively. When they are telling you a story that is shocking, allow the shock to show on your face. Act expressively with your face as an opportunity to show your engagement in what they are telling you and to help communicate on a deeper level.

Facial expressions are mostly accomplished with eyebrows and mouth movements. We will focus more on your mouth in a moment, but in the meantime let's pay attention to how your eyebrows play into the mix. When you are communicating, your eyebrows will often move around to express your thoughts or emotional responses to something someone is sharing with you. One way that you can intentionally manipulate your eyebrows to express interest is to slightly raise them. We tend to raise our eyebrows slightly when we are interested in someone, and especially when they are talking to us. This is almost our way of subconsciously "opening" ourselves to the other person by "opening" our facial expression. If you want to show that you are "open", interested, and engaged, slightly raise your eyebrows when they talk to you.

Smile and Draw Attention to Your Lips

Lips are seductive, especially when we are feeling attracted to a person. Use your lips to your advantage. Smile often, as it shows that you are happy. Not only will they have a positive reaction to your own positive vibes, but the person you are talking to will also be more likely to continue looking at your mouth. Then, you can use other strategies to keep their attention on your mouth. Try subtle things like biting your lip when they are telling you something, licking your lips, or even gently touching them with your fingers.

Drawing attention to your lips means that the person you are flirting with is automatically going to be more interested in them. They may begin to wonder what it would be like to kiss you, or to otherwise be romantically closer with you. Once they *start* thinking on this level, it becomes a lot easier to keep them going down it. Then, you still want to use this strategy to continue keeping your attention on your lips. Don’t overdo it or make it seem like you are obsessively touching your lips as this may be confusing or uncomfortable for the person you are flirting with. However, subtly drawing attention to your lips a few times in each conversation can draw their attention in and create this romantic curiosity that you can then use to help you seduce and date the person you are attracting.

Chapter 4: Don't Be Afraid to Compliment

Compliments are a powerful way to express your interest in someone while also boosting their mood. Naturally, complimenting people is a great way to flirt with them. Not only does complimenting someone increase their attraction toward you, but it also helps them feel more comfortable and confident. Compliments make people feel special and important, this is why they work so well. It is important that if you want to be successful with your flirting, you make use of compliments.

Some people do not like compliments, but you should still give them anyway. These people tend to be the ones that struggle to take a compliment sincerely. This is typically because they are self-conscious or lack self-esteem and self-confidence, therefore they struggle to honestly accept compliments from other people since they don't feel that the compliments are true. When you are flirting, this can tell you a lot about a person. For example, it tells you how they feel about themselves and how well they are at allowing other people to express genuine emotion to that person as well. People who are turned off to compliments may be harder to connect with on a sincere and vulnerable level. For you, learning this about someone gives you the opportunity to decide whether or not you are okay with that. Some people struggle to stay interested in or attracted to people who lack confidence to this degree. Others are not concerned about this and are okay with it.

In addition to letting you know about how a person feels about themselves, compliments also let you tell a person how you feel about them. You can complement people on almost anything. You can complement them on their clothes, their appearance, their physical features (e.g. eyes), their personality traits, or virtually anything else that stands out to you. Compliments should be given freely, but they should be genuine when they are given. Avoid generic compliments whenever possible. This does not mean that you cannot compliment on common things, such as their eyes or their smile, it simply means that when you do it should have sincere emotion behind it. If it doesn't, it will sound like you used the compliment as an ice breaker or for some other reason. When you are flirting, compliments must always be backed by sincere emotion.

There are some things you should consider when you are complimenting someone, especially with the intention of flirting. First, many people compliment others without the intention of flirting. If you are doing it for the intention of flirting, it is important that you make this known. Smile, compliment the person, and use body language signals such as light touch when you are delivering the compliment. This can help them decipher the difference between a friendly compliment and a compliment that was intended to be flirty.

Let's take a look at an example of how you might give a compliment to someone naturally, in a way that shows that you are, in fact, flirting with them:

You are out at a holiday party with your friends. One particular friend that you have known for a long time also happens to be your romantic interest. Only, you aren't sure if they know about it or not. Over the course of the night you find yourself in many friendly situations with this person. You are ready to take the leap, however, and show them how you feel about them. In one conversation, you take the opportunity to invest all of your attention to that person. You talk directly to them, and keep your eye contact on that person. Over time, the other people in the conversation take the sign and wander off. After they have, you see an opportunity to complement their person on their eyes. You slightly lean in, look them directly in the eyes, gently touch their arm and say "Have I ever told you how stunning your eyes are?" You keep looking into their eyes and holding the touch for a few more seconds before letting go.

In this scenario you used a sincere compliment and genuine emotion behind it. Because of that, as well as the body language you used, you made it clear that you meant the compliment in more than just a friendly way. When you are complimenting someone with the intention of being flirty, it is important that you make it clear. You don't want to make a compliment and have it mistaken for friendliness. This may result in you feeling rejected and could reduce your confidence in future flirting endeavors with this particular person.

Another thing to consider when complimenting with people is to make sure that you don't compliment *too* much. Again, when flirting, compliments can be used a lot. However, you want to avoid complimenting someone over and over again without adding any more substance to the conversation. If you flirt too much in this way, you may come off as creepy, someone who lacks social skills, or someone who is desperate. Instead, deliver sincere compliments and balance them out with conversation or alternative flirting strategies.

If you are someone who doesn't personally like receiving compliments, you may find giving compliments harder as well. Something you can do to make it easier is to start small. Begin with easy compliments that you sincerely believe, and work your way up from there. For example, you may find it easier to compliment someone on their outfit or a particular accessory they have rather than complimenting them on their looks or intellect. Once you grow used to giving these types of compliments, look for opportunities to deliver genuine and sincere compliments on more personal subjects, such as their personality or their appearances. The more comfortable you grow with giving compliments, the more comfortable you will likely become with receiving them as well.

Believe it or not, when it comes to flirting there are actually different “standards” when it comes to flirting with each unique gender. Females and males tend to be seduced or turned on by different compliments, which means you may have more success with some over others. In general, men love to be complimented on their appearances and their strengths. Women, however, tend to prefer to be complimented on their intellectual abilities and their knowledge. While men will certainly like being complimented on their intellect and abilities and women complimented on their appearance and strength, the ratio of how many compliments should fall into each category varies for each gender. It can also change from person to person.

Men, in general, prefer to be complimented on their appearances because this is what they use to attract women. This may be because men tend to notice appearances in women more, therefore when a woman takes the time to notice his appearances it is a signal that she must be interested in him. Complimenting a man on his muscles, his outfit, his hair, and his eyes are all great ways to give a genuine compliment that will also leave him feeling especially good about himself. You can also compliment men on their strength, such as how well they can lift things or open things, or how they are capable of physically doing more than you can. These two categories should be the primary categories that you compliment men in. However, ensure that you don’t stay entirely based on image when it comes to compliments. Take the time to compliment a man on his intellect and his personality as well, to avoid making him feel superficial. Even though they are particularly sensitive about their looks, men also like to be commented on their personality and brains. This helps stop them from feeling like all you care about is their look, or like they aren't smart enough for you.

For women, you want to pay attention more to her personality, her intellect, and her smarts. Compliment her on her sense of humor, or how she is brilliant about a particular subject. Women tend to be more attracted to how smart a man is, in addition to how strong he is. For this reason, she is more likely to feel noticed and appreciated if you take the time to pay attention to how smart or charismatic *she* is. Although these should account for the bulk of your compliments, ensure that you compliment a woman on her appearances, too. They often spend a great deal of time ensuring that they look good for special occasions, but they also appreciate genuine compliments about their looks in general. Appreciating her for the effort she puts into her grooming will ensure that you are paying attention and that her efforts are not being wasted.

Chapter 5: Be Happy and Positive

Many people have a tendency to feel nervous and uncomfortable in situations that include flirting, especially if it is with someone new or someone who they like a great deal. A good idea when you are flirting is to create a positive mood for yourself. Be happy, smile, laugh when it is appropriate, and give off a general "good vibe" feel when you are flirting. Not only will this prevent you from nervously rambling or biting your nails, but it will also help make you appear more attractive to the person you are flirting with.

Think about it for a moment: if you were talking to someone who was not positive around you, would you be likely to want to continue being around them? Probably not. Imagine this:

You are at work and you notice how attractive the new guy is. You strike up a conversation with him, hoping to get the opportunity to flirt and leave a lasting impression. As soon as the conversation starts, however, he begins complaining. First he complains about his new job, then he complains about your boss, and finally he complains about what he has to do after work. Although he is physically attractive, you are not interested in listening to his pity party any longer. Suddenly, you no longer feel attracted to him and you are not interested in flirting any longer. Instead, you quickly end the conversation and make a mental note not to talk to him anymore.

When people are nervous, sometimes they have a tendency to ramble on. Often, they will become overly critical of themselves, their life, or their immediate surroundings. This is often because they are feeling nervous and are lacking confidence. Although they may have a perfectly justified reason, however, it is extremely unattractive. People who are excessively negative have a tendency of warding off other people. Because they are always in such a bad mood, people are less likely to want to communicate with them. Instead, they find themselves avoiding that person entirely. While it is completely natural to be in a bad mood at times, you should refrain from taking that bad mood out on the person you are flirting with. In some cases, it may be acceptable to momentarily express your dissatisfaction about something in particular. For example, if you are coworkers and you are mutually complaining about how difficult your boss can be at times, being somewhat negative may be acceptable. However, it is a good idea to refrain from being *too* negative. Furthermore, avoid saying anything excessively harsh about other people, life circumstances, or things. This is unattractive and gives the illusion that you are upset about much more than what you are presently complaining about.

People are naturally attracted to those who are in a positive mood. People who have a positive outlook on life and are generally happy attract more people to them for one very simple reason: people like to feel good. Being positive makes them feel good. When they are in your presence, they find it much easier to be in a positive mood because *you* are in a positive mood. For this reason, you have the power to make them feel better.

When you are being positive, you don't need to be unnaturally positive. Smiling, looking at the bright side of things, finding the silver lining, and otherwise keeping your focus on the positive things in life is a great way to keep your positive spirits without seeming excessively positive. In some instances, people who try too hard to be positive give off a "fake" feeling and other people may not buy into their act. This would be a major turn off, as the person you are flirting with would struggle to trust you and the things you say. Ensure that your positivity and happiness are organic and natural to refrain from being viewed as fake.

Another reason why being positive is important is because it deters those who are not positive. The last thing you want is to find yourself flirting with someone who is excessively negative and who struggles to be positive in their own life. Just as you could drain someone else with your negativity, they may drain you. When you are positive, people who are not naturally inclined to be positive themselves will likely not be overly attracted to you. This is because they are intimidated by your positivity. Instead, they would be more attracted to those who are negative and who lack self-esteem, much like they may.

Being positive works in many ways. If you are currently struggling to be more positive and happy in your own life, know that you are not alone. Furthermore, it is not entirely difficult to start cultivating positivity and happiness in your life. In fact, you have many opportunities to do so on a daily basis! Positivity and happiness are both choices, and you get to choose whether to be positive and happy or negative and upset on a daily basis. Here are some ways that you can choose to be positive and happy each day:

Foster Realistic Positivity

Many people struggle to remain positive because they feel as though they are being dishonest with themselves. They think something such as, "I have a flat tire, what is positive about this?" Being positive doesn't mean that real life doesn't happen to you. It doesn't mean that you say "Wow, a flat tire! How lucky am I?" Instead, it means that you choose a positive outlook even when difficult events take place. For example, you might think "At least I have insurance!" Or, "Hey, I left early for work today. At least I still have plenty of time to get my car to a shop *and* get to work on time!" Be realistic. You are not going to magically be excited about frustrating things just because you choose to be positive. Instead, it simply means that you will choose to see the small shining lights among the difficulties.

People who are not presently living a positive life themselves often think that those who *are* positive don't live within reality. Instead, they might have an illusion that these people somehow believe that every single thing that happens in their life is positive and that there is absolutely no negativity in their world. This is completely untrue. Although it may seem that way to the untrained eye, this is not how positivity works. People who choose to be positive and happy still deal with real, human emotions. They still lose people they love, experience frustrations and disappointments, get their hearts broken, and otherwise deal with painful experiences that are often considered to be "negative". If they are truly choosing to be positive and happy, they will also go through the necessary steps to honestly deal with these emotions, too. If they are angry, for example, they won't suddenly push the anger down in favor of happiness. Instead, they might suppress it for the time being, but once they are in a more appropriate environment they will deal with their anger in a healthy manner. They have chosen to be happy and positive instead, therefore they have also chosen to ensure that the difficult emotions they do experience do not become sources of negativity or pain for them.

If you want to begin being more positive so that you can attract more people into your life, practice waking up and consciously choosing to be positive and happy. When difficult things occur, though, be realistic and honest with yourself. Feel the emotions that arise, work through them, and allow them to naturally subside so that you can resume your positive and happy life. There is no need to be false about your reality or suppress emotions in order to live a truly positive and happy life.

Adjust Your Perception

Although you want to be realistic about how you feel, this doesn't mean you can't be realistic *from a different point of view*. Adjusting your perception surrounding your emotions and how you feel, as well as how you view the things that happen in your life, is a great way to choose to be positive and happy. One great way to adjust your perception is to ask yourself "what is the lesson here?" Virtually everything we experience in life has something it can teach us. Heartbreak and pain can teach us about our own strength, and anger and sadness can teach us about how we react to our environment and what we are dealing with inside of ourselves. Instead of losing yourself in these emotions, find the opportunity to work your way through them while also looking for the lessons that they may be able to teach you.

If you feel that there is no particular lesson to be learned, the lesson itself may be that you need to learn to simply let go. Refrain from dwelling on things and allow them to naturally move by you so that you can move forward in your life. Sometimes, things are not ours to hold on to. Instead, they are simply passing us by on the way to their destination.

In some situations, you may not be able to learn the lesson immediately. For this reason, you should also learn to see the "small victories" in life. For example, say you arrive late for work and so you had to clock in late as well. You know you're going to get in trouble from your boss, so you are stressed out and are not looking forward to dealing with her lecture. You are late because someone hit the back of your car at a red light when they didn't stop fast enough. So, not only are you late, but you also have a major dent in the bumper of your new car. It seems like the bad things just keep piling on, and you are struggling to find any way to be positive among everything that is happening. Instead of getting lost in the frustration, however, you *do* choose to be positive after all. You are grateful that it was only a fender bender and that you weren't hit worse or injured. Furthermore, by removing yourself from the negative situation you enable yourself to talk calmly to your boss, allowing you to explain your situation. Because of your calm and positive demeanor, your boss listens to you and she does not lecture you about being late. Instead, she expresses how grateful she is that you are safe and leaves it at that. As you can see, being positive meant that you were able to find peace and diffuse a potentially negative encounter before it had the chance to turn sour. Changing your perspective not only helps *you* see the good in situations, but it also helps you change how you carry yourself, thus making you more likely to have positive encounters going forward, even after a negative one.

Avoid Labelling Your Thoughts

Something we often do is label our thoughts as "positive" or "negative". When we do this, we actually make it harder for us to be positive. Our thoughts often come to us organically and we have the choice to hold onto them or move them along. If we label them, however, we will likely notice that we have *a lot* of negative thoughts. When we become aware of this, we may start considering ourselves to be negative people. After all, negative people are the ones who have negative thoughts, right? Wrong. Avoid labeling your thoughts and simply work toward consciously choosing which ones you want to keep and which ones you want to let go of.

In addition to being mindful over your thoughts, be mindful over your self-talk, too. Pay attention to how you are talking to yourself as often as possible. Refrain from being overly critical or harsh toward yourself in any way. The way we talk to ourselves has a major impact on how we carry ourselves. If your self-talk is constantly negative, you are going to struggle to be positive. As a result, you will struggle to be positive when you are flirting with people, and this may drive them away.

Feed Positivity with Positivity

Work on boosting your positivity in as many ways as you can. You can feed your positivity by engaging in positive activities, such as exercising and meditating. You can spend time around positive people, and intentionally avoid negative ones. You can also try things such as eliminating negative news programs from your life and reducing the amount of time you spend on social media where negative people tend to flock to. By increasing the positivity in your life and decreasing the negativity, you have a greater ability to increase your own positivity skills.

Feeding your positivity by having a positive environment has a much greater effect on your romantic life than you may think, too. People who are positive when flirting but are surrounded by an enormous number of negative people and energies will often still be a turn off to others who tend to be more positive. This is because the person you are flirting with will likely see through your positive act, assuming that you are only trying to impress them and that you aren't actually being authentic. When you are positive and you surround yourself with positive people and influences, however, you show that you are being authentic and that you are genuinely a positive person. Then, even if you have a somewhat negative day, the person you are flirting with will assume it is just a bad day and that you are generally a happy and positive person.

Being positive and happy feeds every area of your life, but especially the romantic areas. People are attracted to people who are positive. In romance, it shows that you are inspirational, enjoyable, and that you know how to have a good time. It helps lighten the mood, ease the nervous feelings, and help everyone involved feel much happier overall. If you want to have success with flirting, be positive and happy when you are flirting, and build positivity and happiness in your life. This will make it easier to be authentically positive and happy during romantic encounters.

Chapter 6: Don't Take Yourself Too Seriously

Something many people do when they are flirting is taking themselves too seriously. Overthinking, trying to impress the other person, attempting to be positive, and otherwise trying to reinforce their newfound flirting skills can all result in them being far too serious about the situation at hand. Not only does this ruin the mood, but it can also make the person seem either arrogant or unconfident depending on how the seriousness is being displayed.

When you take yourself too seriously, you have a tendency to criticize yourself harshly. You may also get frustrated because you feel that you are not successfully using your flirting strategies. As a result, you end up putting yourself in an unhappy and even downright negative mood. This can ruin the experience for both yourself, and the person you are flirting with. Remember, you want to be positive and happy. Part of being positive and happy is lightening up on yourself and on the person you are with and not taking yourself too seriously.

Another thing that happens when you take yourself seriously is that you come off as pushy and unnatural. Everything from your light touching to your compliments might seem too rehearsed and awkward, making it feel like you are using the other person as a research project instead of genuinely flirting with them. This makes you feel desperate and inexperienced, not attractive and flirtatious. If you take yourself too seriously and you try too hard to flirt properly, you may find that you actually destroy your chances of successfully flirting at all.

Instead, you need to ease up on yourself. Give yourself the benefit of the doubt. Take these steps into mind and use them as guides or points, rather than following them religiously like a step-by-step project. When the moment allows for it, implement one of the skills naturally into the encounter. Don't spend your entire time looking for the opportunities, just let them arise and take advantage of them when they do.

In addition to taking the pressure off of getting every skill right, you should also look for other ways to lighten the mood. Not taking yourself too seriously doesn't only mean that you stop overthinking and putting too much pressure on yourself, but it also means that you take the opportunity to be playful and fun. Playfulness is an extension of positivity and it helps the person you are flirting with feel more attracted to you. It also helps them relax and enjoy the encounter a lot more, too. Make jokes, playfully tease the person you are flirting with, and otherwise poke fun at each other. When they make jokes and tease you back, don't get offended when they do. Let the conversation flow naturally. Show interest in what they enjoy, and look for opportunities to get to know them better.

The best way to take the pressure off and enjoy the encounter for what it is, is to take away any expectations you might have. Don't go into the encounter knowing that you're going to get a phone number or a date unless you have a lot of experience and good reason to believe that the person would agree to either of these things. Instead, see someone you are attracted to and go flirt with them! Smile, laugh, and lighten the mood in any way that you see fit. The more you let things flow and enjoy them for what they are, the more likely they will eventually graduate to something more serious and romantic.

Chapter 7: Leave Them Wanting More

When you are flirting with someone and the encounter is going well, it is likely that you are going to be attentively involved in the conversation and that you will not feel compelled to end it at all. While this is a great sign that attraction is at work, it is also a good sign that you should end the conversation soon. Why? Let's take a look:

You are out on a first date with someone whom you have wanted to date for a long time. As you enjoy your desserts, you notice the conversation getting deeper and deeper. You want to invite them to do something after dinner because things are going so well. It feels like you never want this conversation to end, and you want to know everything that you could possibly know about this person. Instead, however, you finish your dessert and part ways. Because they are so intrigued to learn more about you, they immediately set up date number two. You have left enough to the imagination that they simply must *get to know you better.*

In essence, leaving someone wanting more means keeping parts of yourself mysterious. This mysteriousness helps you keep yourself interesting and keeps the person you are flirting with curious about who you are. Since they already like what they have experienced, they are eager to want to know more. Leaving before the conversation is over means that it feels like things have been left unsaid. The person you are flirting with will likely be interested to learn more about you, therefore they will be more likely to pursue spending time with you again.

Leaving people wanting more puts *you* in charge of the situation. They are so interested in learning more about you that the person will feel strongly about wanting to see you again. People love mystery, and mystery can be created by leaving people hanging. It is as simple as creating a cliff hanger in your conversation and then ending it at that. Because they want to know the answer, they will press you to spend more time together in the future where they will get the opportunity to find out. It’s as simple as that!

Chapter 8: Putting the Steps in Action

In addition to knowing these seven crucial steps to successful flirting, seducing, attracting, and dating, you should also know how to put them into action. Although each chapter explained the steps fairly adequately, understanding how you can amplify your success through these steps will ensure that you have the best chances of succeeding entirely at the art of flirting.

There are a few things that you need to consider when you are implementing these flirting techniques into your own life. Considering these aspects will ensure that you are able to implement these steps without them feeling forced or uncomfortable, or otherwise coming off as desperate or arrogant. Use the following tips to help ensure that you have success with the seven steps of flirting successfully.

Start Slowly

First, you should start slowly when you are learning. Trying to implement too many steps at once could result in you not having great success with the entire process. Instead, it may feel rehearsed and unnatural. The person you are attempting to flirt with may feel uncomfortable, and you may feel as though you are wildly failing. Trying to remember each unique step and the many pieces that go into making it successful all at once can be hard, especially when you are already being faced with the nervousness that naturally arises when we begin flirting with someone.

Instead, start slow. Focus on step one, and take your time mastering it. When you have gotten better and it starts to flow naturally, move on to step two. Continue this slow-moving process until you have completely mastered all of the seven steps. Giving yourself the opportunity to build on your skills in this slower method makes it significantly easier for you to flirt successfully in the end. Although it may take longer for you to get your game up to stride, you will be building it on a solid foundation. That means you are far more likely to avoid any awkward encounters where you may be seen as a “try hard” or someone who is putting in far too much effort to be flirting with someone else. Take your time and practice making these steps and skills come natural to you to increase your success with them.

Practice Where It Doesn’t Matter

There are two reasons why you want to practice where it doesn’t matter: first, it takes the pressure off. When you are flirting with people that you aren’t entirely interested in, it makes it much easier to actually practice the steps of flirting. Because you are not entirely worried about the outcome, you aren't too worried about whether it goes right or not. This means that you start without any overthinking and that you are able to skip directly to the following steps. As you develop more confidence with these steps, it becomes much easier to avoid overthinking in future situations where the flirting actually matters because you are genuinely interested in someone. This does not mean that you should string people along and lead them to believe that you are interested in them, it simply means that you should take advantage of situations that are free of pressure. Use them as an opportunity to increase your flirting skills so that when it *does* matter, you don't feel completely incapable or awkward in the situation.

The second reason why you would want to practice where it doesn't matter is because you don't want to come across as awkward, uncomfortable, under confident, or otherwise unattractive to the person you like. Although this may feel like you are overthinking it, avoiding getting into a situation that you *know* may not go well due to your lack of confidence could result in you further diminishing your confidence. Instead of the situation being empowering and successful, you may end up feeling extremely rejected and therefore like you are completely incapable of flirting with anyone. Starting in an environment where there is no pressure is a great way to build up confidence to have greater success later on in situations where it actually matters.

Understand How Your Entire Life Plays into It

Flirting is important, especially when you are romantically interested in someone. This is, after all, how you let them in on your little secret. However, it is important to understand how your entire life plays into your ability to flirt. This may sound exaggerated, but think about it: if you are extremely under confident in every day social interactions, you are likely to struggle with successfully conveying yourself as confident in flirtatious interactions. Therefore, the best way to increase your skills is to pay attention to how your entire life plays into it. By intentionally building confidence in other areas of your life, such as with your friends, family, and coworkers, you will also increase your confidence in your ability to flirt with other people. This is also true for being charismatic, holding eye contact, not taking yourself too seriously, and following the other important steps of flirting. By increasing your abilities in all areas of your life, you make it much easier for you to have success in flirting specifically.

The best way to determine where you need to improve in life in general is to notice where you struggle most with flirting. If you find you are particularly self-conscious, for example, this may be due to a lack of self-worth. Working toward increasing your self-worth and boosting your self-esteem in all areas of life would then be a great way for you to naturally increase your self-confidence when it comes to flirting. If you find that you are bad at holding eye contact, it may be due to nervousness or anxiety. You would then know that you need to pay attention to all areas of your life and find ways to naturally reduce your nervousness and anxiety overall. For this reason, improving your ability to flirt not only increases your successful flirting interactions, but also improves your charisma and social skills in general.

Improve on Your Own Game

Some people have a tendency to believe that they are masters at flirting. They hit a level of greatness where they have success in most of their initial interactions and therefore they believe that they are naturally incredible and there is nothing that they need to improve on. Unfortunately, this leads to complacency and arrogance. When it comes to anything, including flirting, there is always room for improvement. This is true no matter how good you become.

Flirting is an art, and like any art, you can continually improve on your own skills. Look for opportunities to improve whenever you can. If you notice, for example, you are particularly bad at maintaining eye contact and keeping your full attention on the person you are talking to, practice improving on this particular skill. If you are great at eye contact but find yourself constantly interrupting and trying too hard to impress people, focus on calming down, being positive, and not taking yourself so seriously. No matter how good you are, you can always improve. Even when you are in a relationship, you can improve. In fact, especially when you are in a relationship! Comfort, such as the kind we experience in relationships, tends to lead to us getting complacent and letting our skills go to waste. Don't let that be you! Continue practicing and improving so that you are constantly impressing and attracting your romantic interest to you. This will keep romantic interests engaged and interested in you, no matter how new or old they may be in your life.

Conclusion

Thank you for reading "*How to Flirt: The Right Way*"!

This book was created to help you master the art of flirting the right way in just seven steps. By mastering these seven steps, you can not only improve your ability to flirt, but reap other benefits as well.

I hope that you were able to learn more about the art of flirting and how you can use this handy tool to attract people into your life. By flirting effectively, you not only increase your ability to attract people into your life, but you also make it easier to seduce them and, if applicable, date them!

I also hope that these seven steps were easy enough for you to practice and master so that you can have great success with flirting. Whether you are just looking to have more fun, increase your charisma, or successfully attract the partner of your dreams, I hope you were able to take these steps and generate success using them.

The next step is to ensure that you always work toward improving on your skills. Remember, even if you successfully land yourself in a long-term relationship from these steps, you still need to practice the art of flirting. Flirting is not only great for attracting new partners, but it is also great for keeping our committed partners romantically interested in us. Flirting keeps things fresh, new, and light. Make sure that you are continually working toward improving your game so that you can continually attract your person of interest into your life.

Thank you, and best of luck!

HOW TO
INFLUENCE PEOPLE
THE RIGHT WAY
The Only 7 Steps You Need to Master Persuasion, Manipulation and Impacting People Today
DEAN MACK

BOOK 3: HOW TO INFLUENCE PEOPLE

THE RIGHT WAY

The Only 7 Steps You Need to Master Persuasion, Manipulation and Impacting People Today

Dean Mack

Table of Contents

Introduction

Congratulations on purchasing this book and thank you for doing so.

The following chapters will discuss the 7 most important steps for influencing the people around you. You will learn the best tricks and techniques to master persuasion and manipulation so that others listen to you all of the time.

Getting others to do what you want is not impossible, and you can certainly train yourself to have influence over others. Even if this is not a natural skill that you have, the information provided in this book can teach it to anyone willing to learn.

Many people want to gain control over others only because they want to feel dominant above everyone else. Some people though wants to be influential not because they want to, but because they need to. If you are an employer, a supervisor, or a team manager, or just someone who struggles influencing – or taking control – of others, then this is the perfect book for you.

There are plenty of books on this subject on the market, thanks again for choosing this one! Every effort was made to ensure it is full of as much useful information as possible. Please enjoy!

Chapter 1: Have Confident Body Language

If you want to learn how to influence others, you will first need to know how to portray confident body language. Body language communicates more with others than our words do, and it can make the difference when trying to get others to listen to us. This form of non-verbal communication refers to any expression or gesture that we make to deliver a message to another person.

Oftentimes our body language can make an impression on someone before we get the chance to do so verbally. Imagine walking up to someone that was slumped over with a frown on their face. Your first impression of this person would be that they are upset and sad. Without even talking to the person, you have already drawn your own conclusions about them. This is true for how others view you as well, which is why you want to convey a positive, confident image.

By expanding your body and portraying a confident image, you will alter the way that others view you. Along with this, you will also begin to view yourself in a more positive light and will feel even more powerful in your endeavors to influence other people.

While body language is essential for first impressions, it is also important to maintain confident body language as you carry on a conversation. This is because your body language will help to supplement your spoken message or make it come across more believably. You will need a strong delivery when telling others what you want them to do. Otherwise, they will not take you seriously.

As you come to understand the importance of having proper body language, you must then learn how you can do it yourself. There are many aspects of body language that will matter when trying to influence others, which we will cover.

Your body language should not make it seem as though you are anxious or nervous in any way. You also do not want to make it seem like you are uptight or too serious. To find balance, you should watch yourself in the mirror and critique your own body language. As you go through each aspect of body language to improve upon, you can practice in a mirror until you feel ready to use it around someone else. You will need to make sure that you seem natural, but also somewhat intimidating so that others still take you seriously.

To begin identifying areas that you should improve on in terms of body language, start by looking at your posture. Posture will be the key to how you carry yourself for when others begin to form an opinion of you. To work in this area, start by pressing your chest slightly outward and moving your stomach in. Keep your shoulders held back and keep your head up. Be sure to check yourself in a mirror to make sure that you are not overextending any part of your body so that you still look as natural as possible. Practice holding this position frequently until it becomes natural. Over time, you will find that your body will naturally sit this way without you having to think about it or look in a mirror.

Keeping your head up high is essential for good posture, but is also going to be a large determining factor on how others perceive you. If you are keeping your head down, you are indicating that you are not the one in control of the conversation or situation. By keeping your head up, you make it possible to take control of a situation so that you can start to influence those around you and convey confidence in your abilities to do so.

Once your posture is sufficient, you may then begin to work on your eye contact. Sometimes maintaining eye contact with others can feel awkward or intimidating, but you can get past these feelings to influence others. You should focus on keeping eye contact with other people in every conversation you have. This will make people respect you more and will let them know that you are still listening to what they have to say. If someone does not think you are listening to them, they will be less likely to care about what you are saying in return and will be harder to influence.

You should also take care to not offer too much eye contact, as this can be too aggressive and may seem strange to the other person. If the other person feels threatened by you, they are not any more likely to listen to you than if you had not maintained any eye contact at all. Again, you will need to practice this skill and become more conscious of it in each conversation that you have.

Now that you have learned how to master proper posture and eye contact, you will also need to learn how to form sufficient gestures. The most common ones that you will utilize are smiling and handshakes, so learning these first is essential.

The most important thing to note for smiling to influence others is that you must time it appropriately. Smiling can be your most powerful method of influence or your most dangerous one, depending on how you go about it. You do not typically want to walk into a crowded room with a smile on your face immediately. You first want people to recognize your attendance and build a presence in the room. Once there has been an opportunity for this, you can smile as you wish. Be sure to smile when it is fitting, such as for excitement or in a positive interaction. You also want to be sure that your smiles are natural and legitimate, as it is often easy to see through a fake smile. By mastering this, others will feel connected to you and will be more likely to be influenced by you later on.

As for handshakes, you will need to convey a sense of power. A firm and strong handshake will immediately grab the attention of others when you greet them, as it shows that you respect them, as well as yourself. You may also want to be the first one to initiate the handshake, as this conveys a sense of authority to the other person that may be difficult to obtain otherwise. For example, if you are about to interview for a position, you may benefit from extending your hand first so that you are one step ahead of the interviewer, which they are likely to respect whether they are cognizant of it or not. Once you have started the handshake, allow it to last for up to about 5 seconds before pulling away.

Fidgeting may also be an issue that you struggle with when it comes to confident body language. People who are nervous tend to move their hands or their bodies without purpose, which is easily noticed and does not give off a professional vibe. You may need to consciously find a place to put your hands or a position that you do not move back and forth in to halt any nervous movements you might be doing. Take careful note of when these movements are happening so that you may pinpoint why and what you can do to stop them. For example, if you are someone that plays with their hair when nervous, you may find that tying your hair back stops you from doing this. You may also be doing this because it puts you at ease, but others can recognize it as nerves that are making you do it.

You will also need to make sure that your body language shows that you are engaged. This will be accomplished somewhat with smiling and eye contact, but there are extra steps you should take as well. To do this, you want to make sure that you are reacting while listening to a conversation. As mentioned, the other person must recognize that you are listening to them before they will be willing to listen to you. You can accomplish this by nodding throughout the conversation, as well as mirroring any movements or expressions made by the other person. The movements that they are making reflect how they feel, and by doing a similar movement, you will show them that you feel a similar way and that you recognize their feelings.

Purposefully utilizing your arms and legs will also be important for body language. Even if you are not using your arms or legs to communicate, their placement will be essential to the vibe that you are giving off. For example, if your arms are crossed over your chest during a conversation, you are suggesting that you feel uncomfortable or that you do not like talking to the other person. To avoid this, you can first become more aware of where your arms and legs are. By recognizing their placement, you can learn to adjust accordingly. You can place your arms on your side or keep your legs crossed to look relaxed and engaged. However, you will need to remember to keep your placements natural as well. Otherwise, it will negate your efforts to show that you are involved and interested in the conversation.

After reviewing all of the previous information on body language, you should also take time to note the culture you are in and what is considered to be acceptable. Every culture has their own forms of body language that are considered professional or friendly, so you will need to be careful to not come off the wrong way. There are also some forms of body language that are disrespectful, which will also be important to learn about. If you are interacting in a setting that may have a different style of body language from what you are used to, you will need to acclimate yourself to the rules of that culture so that you are still able to influence others effectively. For example, in the United States, maintaining proper eye contact is important, as we already covered. However, you would not want to utilize the same eye contact principles in Japanese culture. This is because Japanese people tend to only make eye contact at the beginning of a conversation and find it awkward to maintain it from there. You would not be as likely to have influence over another person in this culture if you tried to make the same amount of eye contact as you do in the United States.

Body language is an essential skill that you must learn if you want to have influence and power over other people. This form of communication is crucial in making an impact on others so that they will listen to you and respect you. Once you have mastered this skill, you will be ready to move forward in the process of influencing people effectively.

Chapter 2: Make People Like You

When you meet someone for the first time, you may find it hard to remember what they looked like or what they said. However, you are far more likely to remember how that person made you feel. Whether they made you feel nervous or happy, your memories and impressions of the person are based on how you felt when talking to them.

The next step in learning to influence others is to make people like you. You will need to learn how to make good impressions so that you are memorable and respected enough to be listened to.

One of the main factors in how likable you are is your charisma. This charm to your personality is what will attract others so that they are drawn in and open to listening to what you have to say. Most of us have some room for improvement in this area, which is why it should be the first consideration when trying to make others like you.

To become more charismatic, you should first attempt to make yourself more present. As we covered in the last chapter, engagement during a conversation is incredibly important. This is true even now, as getting rid of any distractions will be appreciated by the other person that you are talking to. When your full attention is in the conversation, it becomes yours to control. Because people desire attention, providing this when communicating gives you the upper hand so that you may begin to influence in whatever way you choose.

Another way to be charismatic is to be sure that you are not focusing on your response while someone else is talking. This goes along with making sure your full attention is in the conversation, but can still be easy to forget. The tendency to think about own responses is hard to ignore, but it distracts from what is being said and shows that you are not listening as much as you should be. It is alright to think about your response when the other person has stopped talking, and will even give you a better opportunity to collect your thoughts and consider everything they said so that your response is appropriate. This will also be much more appreciated and will enhance the communication for you to influence.

The main goal of being more charismatic is to make people feel good. When you have this power over people, the rest of the influencing you do becomes much easier. However, there are still many other ways to make people like you to influence them as well.

One of the ways to make people like you more is to demonstrate power over them. Most people respond well to authority figures, although this may not work for everyone you encounter. However, you may notice that people give into you much more easily and do as you say.

To convey a sense of power, you should first double check your body language. As we covered in the previous chapter, this will be your first impression on others and can give you a head start on gaining power and making people like you. Once this has been accomplished, you can start finding other ways to gain power over others.

One simple way to demonstrate power in a situation is to take control of the environment. This can be moving the objects around you or being the first one to initiate a conversation. While you do not want to be fidgeting too much when doing this, it is ok to pick up an item or two just to show that you can. You may also try initiating a handshake to establish power in your situation. You can be creative with this task and adjust it as needed to your environment.

People will also like you more when you are humble. While you do not want to sell yourself short, it is important to respect the knowledge that others can give to you. Even if you are influential, you will still need to learn from other people and acknowledge what they can offer you.

Practicing humility will also include praising others. People like to know that they are doing a good job and that you think highly of the work that they do. By demonstrating this, others will like and respect you more. You will need to give people the credit that they deserve for what they do if you ever want to have any influence over them. Imagine having a boss that took all of the credit for the work that you did and never praised you for doing any of it. While the boss might still have actual power over your job, they would likely have little influence over what you did otherwise because you do not get the credit that you deserve for your work. Anyone would feel underappreciated and resentful in a situation like this one.

Another piece of advice for being humble is to take a step back. This means allowing others to speak more and allowing them to do something first. You may be eager to talk or do everything you can when trying to gain influence, but this can often hinder your ability to do so. It also helps to give others the perception that they are the ones in control of a situation, which being humble will help with. If performed correctly, the other person will do most of the talking and will go first in any tasks that need to be completed. This will give you the chance to listen to them and pay attention to what matters. They will also like that they feel in control and will also feel more connected with you.

Do not be afraid to admit your mistakes. This is another part of practicing humility because you must recognize when you are wrong and have messed up. It is hard for people to like being around someone who thinks that they are always right and do not know when to admit that they are wrong. If you are conscious of this and attempt to do it yourself as often as possible, you will notice that others are appreciative of it.

Another way to get people to like you more is to be positive. Your mood and emotions have a powerful influence on others that they likely do not even notice. When you are happy and positive, those around you will start to become this way as well. You will also notice that people are attracted to you more when you are positive, and they will also be more willing to listen to you. Do not be afraid of displaying happiness around other people, even if their mood is somewhat down. They will soon begin to reflect your good mood subconsciously, which will give you the upper hand to be the one with power in the situation.

Being more positive might also involve making other people laugh. There is a time and place for joking around, but sometimes it is a good way to get people to like you. It can lighten the mood and make others feel more comfortable around you. Be sure to tell jokes that are appropriate for the situation. No one wants to hear a sexual joke during a serious conversation, and it is a quick way to ruin your credibility. Timing will be everything with this suggestion, so be sure to use it wisely.

You will also find that sharing common traits with others makes them like you more as well. These traits can be good or bad, as either way will form a connection. Humans are attracted to people that are similar to them, so identifying characteristics, traits, and qualities that you have in common with someone else will instantly make them like you more. This is one of the most important ways to make people like you more and can be used on just about any person you meet. No matter who they are, you will have at least one or two things in common with them that you can bond over. By making this connection, you will be more likable and will gain influence as needed.

When people like you they are more likely to listen to you. This may seem obvious, but it is not always be easy for everyone to accomplish. Some have the natural talent of walking into a room and making everyone they meet enjoy their company. Even if this isn't you, it is possible to make it happen.

All of the previous bits of information will help you get people to enjoy being around you in just about any situation. You will need to make people feel good and validated in your communications with them and show that you are humble and respect them as well. The more interested that you are in other people, the more interested they will be in you.

Once you have learned and practiced all of the suggestions outlined in this chapter, you will be ready to move on to become more concise and clear to gain influence over others.

Chapter 3: Be Clear and Concise

Persuading others can be a daunting task, and it is easy to be a bit nervous when trying to do so. However, there are a few ways that you can prepare yourself so that your persuasive skills work. The most important way being that your words need to be both clear and concise, as the chapter title indicates. This may take some work, but once mastered it will be one of the most effective ways to influence other people.

This chapter might take you back to the writing classes you took in school, as the learning principles are similar. It can often be difficult to translate what we want to say into actual words, such as with writing or speaking. By exploring ways of going about this, you can become a much better talker so that others do what you say.

To start becoming clearer when you speak, you will need to not be so "wordy." This means to simplify most of the verbs that you use, or any sentences in general. You may tend to use abstract phrases or terms when you want to sound smart, but this is unnecessary. If anything, doing this makes it obvious to the other person that you are trying to impress and influence them. You also run the possibility of misusing words or stumbling over phrases, thus losing your credibility even if you had previously been successful.

To practice simplifying what you say, pay attention to the verbs that you are using. For example, instead of saying “Her movements are suggestive of...” you could say “Her movements suggest...” in place of the other verbiage. A change like this may seem insignificant, but it makes more message clear without any extra “fluff” added on to it. The example given is also just a small bit of a phrase, as you will have more than just a word or two to alter.

Simplifying your message should also include using more active verbs instead of passive. Examples of passive words include “we have” and “there are.” Instead, you should declare what you want as you speak. An example of an active sentence would be, “I believe that we must place the dresser on the right side of the bed.” The previous example conveys what you want and not that it “should” or “could” be done. You do not have to sound demanding with this kind of verbiage, but you demonstrate your own decisiveness and give a simple command of what you want.

Another way you can simplify your words is to work on using fewer vague phrases and nouns. By using vague words, you draw yourself into saying even more to make up for it so that your message still makes sense. Some examples of vague words include area, place, situation, aspect, degree, and consideration. An example of a vague phrase you might use would be, “Let’s go to that place across the street with good tacos.” Instead of saying the previous sentence, you could say, “Let’s go to the taco restaurant across the street.” You may be using vague words without realizing it, so you may need to analyze how you speak frequently. It is hard to change how you speak when you have been doing it for a long time, but it will pay off. What you say will be clear and to the point, minus all of the unnecessary verbiage you were using previously.

Once you have cleaned up what you say, you can start to make your words more concise. This step is equally as important as clarity, as the two together will make you much more respectable and persuasive. The overall goal is for you to make your messages quick and understandable so that people listen and remember what you say. Being concise means that you are going to use a few words to say a lot. This also means that you will need to choose your words wisely.

To be concise, the most important step you can take is to think before you say anything. This will allow your words to feel more natural, but also considerate and necessary. This will allow you the opportunity to compose your thoughts and sort them down into a simple message. You do not want to take more than 5 seconds to do this, as this would often make the situation awkward. However, these few seconds are all you need to stop yourself from blurting out the first words that come to your mind. Instead, you will be able to say what you mean without filler.

The next way to make what you say more concise is to start and end with your main idea. Humans tend to remember the beginning and the end of what we are taught. For example, in a lecture, you might remember what was said initially and right before you left, but a lot of what was said in between might be hard to remember. Given this, it is important to remember when speaking so that you can plan your words accordingly. You should start and end with the most important concepts so that people remember what matters. This will also help to guide your listeners and make them think about what you are saying. By introducing them early to what you want, it becomes more memorable, and they are more likely to do it.

Once you have mastered getting your most important concepts and desires out first and reiterating them at the end, you need to learn what to say in between so that people still listen to you. The middle of your message should still consist of important information, but only that which supports the main idea. This should include only the most important details and nothing that could be written off as irrelevant. You need to allow yourself to give the most effective communication possible to get people to listen to you and remember what you say.

Paying attention to your filler sounds while talking is important as well. You need to 'clean up' your sentences and avoid the 'ums' and 'ohs' that tend to happen that hinder the effectiveness of what you are saying. You should practice speaking on your own time to observe how often you make these noises while talking so that you can work on stopping them. These noises also delay you from getting to the point of your message, which is distracting for your audience. A lot of this is avoided by taking time to think about what you are going to say, but may still be difficult to avoid without practice.

While having a clear, concise message is vital to getting people to do what you want, you must also be sure to tailor your message to your audience. The suggestions outlined in this chapter would likely not be the way you would talk to a friend in a casual setting, but it would be if you were trying to get them to do something for you. You should identify who you are talking to and what it is that they need to know. Knowing your audience will help you to avoid awkward communication and will allow you to figure out how much you should say.

As previously stated, knowing your audience will help you to determine what they need to know from you. However, to accomplish this, you must first know what you want to say. You should always know the 'why' for what you want to say so that you can plan your message and make it as effective as possible. You are wasting your own time if you do not even know what and why you want to influence other people, and they will also not respond well. Sometimes the reason why you want something to happen is obvious, but some cases might require some analyzation. You should take time before your interactions with others to make sure that you are serious and know the reasons why you want to influence. If you are not absolutely certain, you will not be successful.

The last tip for improving your speaking and communication to be more concise is to stay focused. Your undivided attention should be on your interaction and the goals you want to achieve from it. You already know the ‘why’ for trying to influence someone to do something, and you must keep that in mind. Be sure to not get distracted as you speak and start to go off on an unnecessary tangent. You want people to take you seriously, so you must be serious about it as well.

Once you have reviewed the information in this chapter, you will become a more effective speaker. You also now understand the importance of good communication so that others will listen to you and do what it is that you want. Influencing others becomes much easier when your communication skills are strong.

The more you explore how to improve communication, the more you can influence others. This may be an obvious change you can make, but there are also less obvious changes as well. In the following chapter, we will explore one of these less obvious changes, which is to ask others for favors.

Chapter 4: Ask for Favors

Influencing people will require you to be somewhat manipulative when talking. While manipulating might not be the most ethical way to go about getting what you want, it can prove to be advantageous overall. You can also go about it a positive way.

Manipulation can be done in a variety of ways, some better than others. One of those ways, which is also one of the most effective, is to ask people for favors.

It might sound counterintuitive, but asking for favors makes people perceive you more positively. It even makes you seem like a more influential person. This is a phenomenon called the "Ben Franklin Effect."

Essentially, this effect is described as when a person does a favor for someone else, they become more likely to do more favors for that same person in the future. The thought behind this is that we internalize helping out the other person was because we like them already. This makes sense because we tend to only do extra favors for those that we like, whereas we would not be as willing to do the same for someone we dislike.

This effect is useful in a variety of situations. Imagine being in a business setting where you are trying to get a client to purchase your product. Instead of offering your own assistance to this client, you can ask them to do something for you. For example, you can ask them to tell you their opinion on where the market is heading and what exactly they would want from an ideal product. With this favor going unrepaid, they are likely to do more for you in the future. They will be more likely to give you their time and investments, possibly even purchasing the product from you.

Another term for a similar effect is the "foot in the door" technique. This one is described as asking someone to do a somewhat small favor for you so that they are more willing to do a large favor for you in the future. This one is attributed to what social scientists refer to as "successive approximations."

When a person does a lot of small favors for you, they notice a behavior or attitude change in you that is typically positive. To stop this from turning negative, they will agree to do larger favors for you after doing multiple small ones so that they do not let you down. This is a common business technique but can be used in your own life. If a salesperson comes knocking on your door and asks if you would allow them to come inside, this is likely just the first in a long succession of favors that will be asked of you.

These effects only emphasize the importance of Chapter 2, which describes how to get people to like you. That initial familiarity will be important and will almost guarantee that the other person will agree to that initial, small request.

It may seem weird that people actually enjoy doing favors for one another. We enjoy helping out the people we like, you just need to know the right way to go about asking someone to do something for you.

While you may now understand why asking for a small favor and then a big favor helps you to get what you want, you should also know how to go about asking for these favors. It can be a little awkward to ask people for something, especially if you have tried to avoid doing so in the past. You may be uncomfortable with the idea, but there are appropriate ways to approach people that will help you ease into it.

To go about asking for a favor, you can start by planning to do it at the right time. You want to be courteous to the person you are asking the favor of, as you want to make it seem as tiny of an inconvenience as possible for them. If the timing is wrong, they may be unable or annoyed that you requested anything. Try to find the best time to do so and in the right setting. You do not want to ask a professor to help you with an assignment in the middle of a lecture, and you do not want to ask a friend to borrow something of theirs when you are out with a group of friends. Avoid putting the person in an awkward situation so that they are open to helping you out, no matter what the favor may be.

While asking for a favor should be considerate, you also do not want to state that you are bothering someone by asking them. This immediately looks bad on you and enables the other person to have full control of the situation. It is not bothersome to ask a favor of someone, as we already covered how people actually enjoy doing favors and get pleasure from it.

You also do not want to be sneaky about your intentions when asking for something. It is courteous to let the other person know that you are seeking a favor right away, that way they do not have to figure out what you are trying to get from them. It prepares the other person to consider your request, instead of being surprised by it later. You are also more likely to be rejected if you ask after a long conversation that was leading up to the question. It is best to start off by saying you are looking for a favor and then just asking!

The wording of your request will be vital to success as well. You want to be careful with how you pitch your request, being sure that it is polite and gracious to the other person. After all, they are the one helping you out, so you do not want to be perceived as rude. You also do not want to create any confusion or misunderstandings, so you want to word your request as simple as possible. An example of a simple and polite request would be, "Do you mind sparing about an hour of your time to come to my place and help me study for my Spanish exam?" While specific, the previous example is simple and is considerate of the time you will be taking away from the other person.

As mentioned, you do not want to be rude at all to the person you are asking a favor of. You want to be as polite as possible during the encounter. One way you can go about doing this is to flatter them a little. You do not want to compliment them excessively or to exaggerate their skills, as they can easily see through this. For example, do not tell someone you are seeking their help because they are the best at Algebra, especially if it is not something that they actually excel in. Instead, you can just say that you want their help because you know they are good at it and that you can stand to learn from someone like them. You should also thank them to show your appreciation. Even if they decline to assist you, thanking them shows that you still respect their decision either way. This may also help you in the future if you ask them for help again, as they will be more likely to accept given how polite you were this time.

Along with flattery and being thankful, you also want to make sure that you follow through on any commitments you have made with your requests. For example, if you asked to borrow an item and gave a time frame for returning it, you need to follow through. Getting the item back promptly shows the other person respect and makes them trust you more in the future.

One of the last things to know about asking favors is to offer a way out for the other person. As much as you want the other person to accept your favor, you need to know how to accept a no. You also need to make it possible for them to decline so that they do not feel pressured to accept something they do not want to do. Be sure to note your understanding at the end of your request if they choose to not do whatever you are asking. Also make sure to mention that it is alright if they feel uncomfortable or are unable to accept your request, as this will put them at ease. No one enjoys doing a favor that they feel like they were forced to do, and they will surely not want to do more for you in the future. If you have to force someone into doing something for you, you do not have true influence. It is not hard to gain actual power, at least not compared to the influential power that you can gain over people with skill.

Giving is often more fulfilling than receiving, which is why people are so willing to help each other out. Even if you struggle to get others to do things for you now, this is a skill that you can practice to manipulate others.

When people already like you, it is easy to get them to do favors for you. From there it is all about how you approach the situation and what methods you use to ask. Do not be afraid of asking others for something, as you can get what you want.

You can also get what you want by building your relationships with other people. Sometimes it is not enough for them to just like you and it may require a special emotional connection. We will discuss the best way to go about building this kind of connection in the following chapter.

Chapter 5: Make Emotional Connections

The focus of this chapter is on the emotional connections you make with people to impact them and influence. We have briefly covered this topic before, but this chapter will give you more insight as to how you should build connections and why it is important in influencing other people.

When you are trying to influence others, you may be delivering sensitive or important information to get people to want to do it. This can be an advantage point though, as you should build an emotional connection with the people you are interacting with. This goes hand in hand with making people like you but takes it a little further.

There is a lot of psychological background to this step that suggests its credibility, much of which was researched by John Medina. It has been shown that people 'tune out' of conversations after just a few short minutes and do not retain information if it was boring and uninteresting. To avoid this, you have to build connections with people and make them interested in what you have to say. The way to do this is to get the chemical called dopamine pumping through the person you are interacting with. This chemical is what allows us to feel pleasure and enjoy being around other people. If you can stimulate this part of the brain, you can gain power over others to influence them.

If you want people to listen to you and want to build meaningful connections with them, you will need to start your conversations off strong. You want to grab the attention of the other person and immediately make them feel wanted and important. One of the best ways to do this is to start off with a question or comment that involves the other person. For example, you might start off by asking, "How was your day?" or "What was the most interesting part of your day?" You want the other person to feel as special as possible and grab their attention. When they recognize that you care about them, they will instantly feel more connected and ready to listen.

Another way to build an emotional connection with someone to influence them is to involve them as much as you can in the conversation. You should ask questions and gain the perspective of the other person on what you are discussing. You can also try to analyze their feelings and judge how willing they are to do what it is that you are wanting. Asking questions also makes the other person feel understood and listened to. You should show the other person recognition and show that their thoughts are being considered as well. By doing this, they will like being around you more and will begin to feel much more appreciated. When others feel important, they will be easily influenced.

All of that which has been said thus far is to help you build rapport with the people you want to influence. This is vital to your success, as this connection will make them more likely to do tasks for you. Do not be afraid to get these people talking about themselves. Be sure that you are listening as they talk and are engaging them as much as possible. Learn about these people at any opportunity that is given to you so that you can make comments about their interests along the way. You want to make sure that you make them feel special and that you care about what they do. If you want people to respect and be impacted by you, they must feel a connection.

Another simple way to build emotional connections is to remember the other person's name. This is a small, yet important detail when trying to influence someone. While it may not seem like much when you remember a name, not remembering can have many negative effects that will be hard to come back from. You want to be able to say the other person's name regularly so that they feel validated and remembered. By not remembering, the other person senses that you do not truly care and that you cannot even remember the small things about them. If this is the perception that they have, then they will likely not do anything for you.

We have already covered the importance of being positive around others to get them to do what you want, but you should also look for the positives in them. It is a natural tendency to be somewhat cynical and not immediately see the good in people, but there is plenty of good to look for. If you want to be successful in building emotional connections, you will need to master looking for this. Be sure to focus on reasons to like them and set aside any reasons you may not want to be around them. This will help you to expect the best out of people, which they will then deliver once the connections are made.

When trying to make emotional connections with people, you expect them to open up to you a bit. This is how you will build trust with them and make the connections real. It is important that they open up to you and do not regret it later on. You want to avoid mocking or making the other person feel judged, thus regretting showing that side of them to you. If this happens, it is highly unlikely that they will be strongly influenced by you anymore and they may try to even do the opposite of whatever you say. Instead, you should try to empathize with them and their beliefs. Even if you do not agree with what they do, empathy can show that you respect their decisions to do something a certain way and even gives you the chance to reveal more about yourself. You want to be open and non-judgmental so that people trust you and are not afraid to be themselves around you. Without this quality, people will not listen to you or be influenced by what you say.

Getting a little personal will also help you to build a connection with others. We have already stated that you should ask questions to try to get to know someone, but do not be afraid to dig a little deeper than superficial questions. When someone tells you what they do for a living, try to ask why they chose that profession or what made them want to do that. This will help them open up to you and reveal more about themselves that you might not have otherwise known. You can learn what they care about and what makes them tick. This will also give you the chance to show your passions so that there is mutual respect, which will then give you the opportunity to have a higher impact on them later on.

Along with everything else you do to connect to people, the most important thing that you can do is to treat people the way that you would want to be treated. This is the 'golden rule' for being nice to others, one that you may have been taught from a young age. You will show a lot of deserved respect to the other person when you follow this rule, as no one wishes to be treated poorly. You will also find that you want to listen to them even more and gain their insight, such as you would if the tables were turned.

It is also worth mentioning that you should not try to 'one-up' someone when building connections and friendships with them. As people tell you about themselves, be sure to not use it as an opportunity to brag about yourself and your accomplishments. While self-disclosure is necessary and assists in building relationships, you do not want to overdo it. The point is to influence other people and learn about them. If you are too focused on yourself, all of your other attempts will have been for nothing. Make sure you are taking time to listen and build the connection effectively and without selfish causes.

Influencing others will require you to connect with others and build strong relationships with them. We listen to the people that we respect the most and feel comfortable with. You should utilize this fact to your own advantage so that you gain power over people and can have an impact on them. You want people to perceive you as approachable so that they can come to you with requests, which you can then ask for in return later on.

There are many advantages to connecting with other people, the most obvious one being the power that it gives you to them. By reading the information in this chapter, you are well prepared to start improving your connections with people and use them to influence as you want.

In the next chapter you will learn how to use your connections that you have built and to become more transparent to other people. This will provide you even more power to influence others and to have an impact on the lives of others.

Chapter 6: Be More Transparent

To be persuasive and get people to do what you want, you need to be vulnerable and make your intentions clear. We touched upon this topic when learning how to ask for a favor, as you want to make it apparent what you want right away.

You may wonder why you should be transparent about your intentions when trying to get what you want from others. Doesn't this take away from the manipulative aspect of influencing? Maybe so, but being transparent actually helps to get other people to do what you want. Being open and vulnerable increases your likability, and therefore your influence. People like to see your emotions, and they will also trust you more when doing so. Most people assume you would not show them your vulnerable side if you did not like or trust them in return.

Being transparent also means being able to admit your mistakes. Admitting to your own flaws and weaknesses shows the other person that you are 'real' and are an equivalent to them. They can relate to you on a more personal level when you display emotions and admit to your weaknesses. This will get them to trust and like you even more, thus resulting in a higher ability to influence on your end. You do not want to make yourself seem perfect out of fear that others will think less of you. We are all only human, and we all know that each person messes up from time to time, so do not be afraid to own up to this fact.

To start being more transparent, remember to make your intentions obvious from the start. If you plan on asking someone something, let them know immediately. If you just want to talk to that person and spend time with them, make this obvious as well. Do not leave your audience guessing what it is that you want, as this decreases their willingness to give it to you.

You also need to learn how to be open with others. This does not mean you have to reveal every intricate detail of your life, but you should not be afraid to open up. You want people to be able to read you so that they trust you and everything that you say. Think about what others might find interesting to know about you and tell them! You would be surprised at the connections this will help you build and how much others will respect how vulnerable you make yourself.

To be open with others, you should tell a story about yourself that demonstrates what kind of person you are. You might select a funny story or a vignette about your day that gives them a snapshot of your life. No matter what instance you choose, you want it to reflect who you are. It does not hurt to add something in that makes the other person smile, as well as something to personalize the story that shows your character. The purpose of this is to tell the other person more about yourself, so be as detailed as necessary. Of course, you should only use this tip if the timing is right and if it is warranted. You will need to be your own judge of this, but do not be afraid to utilize this helpful strategy.

Being transparent can also involve sharing your thoughts and opinions on topics, even if they are controversial. You do not want to bite your tongue all of the time if you desire to be impactful. You should know your stance on a subject and be able to back it up. People will respect that you know your stance and are well-educated enough to discuss it openly. Even if you do not think others will agree with you, it is ok to share your thoughts on a subject. You should still be respectful of other people's opinions and not think less of them if they disagree with you. This allows people to see your way of thinking and get an idea of how your mind works.

You can also be more transparent by keeping people in the loop about your life. When people like you, they will take a genuine interest in your life, and you should be willing to let them know more about yourself. For example, if you have been working on a blog or searching for a new job, other people might be interested to know this about you. This makes it easy for other people to engage you in conversation and find out more. They may also be more likely to get involved with what you are doing and want to take part in it, which may be a potential benefit to you as well.

One of the most obvious, yet often overlooked, aspects of transparency is honesty. While what we have covered so far implies that making yourself vulnerable involves being honest about yourself with others, it does not hurt to remind yourself of this as well. You do not want to hide who you are from other people, as they will never trust you. Do not be afraid to share your honest opinions and thoughts, even when others do not agree. You will be more successful in earning respect by sharing what you think without trying to cover it up anyway. This can be scary for some people, as we often put a filter on ourselves to avoid judgment. As long as you approach each situation the right way and create an environment of mutual respect, you should have no problem being honest to become more transparent.

Along with being honest, you should also take care not to give people a false sense of hope or provide pretenses. This is a part of being honest, but can still be a cause of a misunderstanding. Sometimes just the tone of voice or way you approach a situation can give people the wrong idea and make them expect something that might not be guaranteed. For example, if you are a boss at your company and you always approach one of your employees in a cautious, friendly manner, they might not realize when an issue has become serious. Even if you have redirected them in the past, the way you approached the situation might have been misleading for them. Do not assume that people will always understand your meaning, as this can cause miscommunication. Instead, be honest and upfront about everything. Do not try to "sugarcoat" anything, especially not when it is something important. You want people to be able to not only hear but also to see your intentions, no matter what the situation is.

When being transparent, you should take caution not to come off as self-centered. Of course, this step requires you to talk about yourself, but you must know the limits. Do not spend the entire conversation talking about yourself and your own emotions. Be sure to involve the other person and ask questions about them as well, just as you learned from previous steps. Even if they are not being as transparent about themselves as you are, it is good to offer them the opportunity to share after you have revealed more about yourself.

Transparency and vulnerability will assist you in your endeavors to be influential. These are the qualities you need to get people to listen and care about what you say, as they show that you have absolutely nothing to hide. This is a technique that the greatest of leaders use to get people to trust them and to make their disciples like them. Transparency and vulnerability also have the benefit of improving your friendships and relationships, as these traits are appreciated by just about everyone you will meet.

People will also feel more connected to you when you make yourself vulnerable to them. As we have covered before, this feeling of closeness will make them more likely to do what you want, which has been the overall goal for each of these steps.

In the next chapter, we will cover how to take an interest in others to gain influence, as this chapter has mostly revolved around getting people to know more about you. These steps, in combination with everything else that has been covered, will get you much closer to being an influential person.

Chapter 7: Take an Interest in Others

A lot of this book has focused on working with others. After all, you can only influence people that are willing to listen to you. This chapter will reiterate this important fact and help you to work even better with other people.

People want to feel liked and respected, as we have discovered. It cannot be underestimated how being nice to others will get you what you want. Part of being nice to others will also require you to take an interest in others.

We already know that we should ask questions and pay full attention when other people are talking to us. You can also do a lot to show that you are attentive and listening, such as making appropriate eye contact.

Along with what has been covered so far, there are many other ways that you can show your interest in others. One of these ways is to learn how to read people.

Every person has different qualities and practices that will be influenced in different ways. It will be your job to figure out how each person works so that you can read what will work on them.

To read people, you should start by paying attention to their body, both language, and characteristics. This will indicate a lot about their current emotions and will tell you what they are feeling. For example, if the person has their arms crossed and looks away from you, they are probably not in a great mood. You might also notice any tattoos they have or a special ring that they are wearing that you might comment on. You can learn a lot about a person just based on what they wear and how they carry themselves, so be sure to note these things when interacting with someone.

Reading people will also involve paying attention to the emotions that they are trying to show you. While some of this is readable from body language and appearance, you will also be able to sense emotions. Intuition will be used to understand what other people are feeling, and you should be sure to consider this and obvious signs that they are conveying. For example, when you meet someone, you should think about how they are making you feel. Do you feel delighted to be around them or do you feel somewhat uncomfortable? How you feel is often based on the vibe that the other person is giving off, which might be responded to by your subconscious mind. You should also pay attention to their tone of voice and laughter as they are talking, which will convey their emotions. You may notice that some people get a higher pitched voice when they are nervous or that their voice tends to shake around certain topics. Making note of this is important because you will be able to tell what they are feeling based on these sounds.

When trying to read someone you should also notice the spacial differences between the two of you. You can tell if someone is interested in talking to you based on how far away they sit or stand. The person may not necessarily have something against you personally even if they are standing far away, but it does give you an indication that something is not right. It could be that they do not want to feel intimate or vulnerable at that time, or perhaps they are more of an introverted person in general and do not want to be close physically.

By learning how to read others, you take an interest in what they are feeling and how they act around you. You can also show your interest by offering compliments to the people you talk to. Not only does this make them feel good about themselves, they recognize that you pay attention to them. It is best if the compliments that you give are based on qualities or characteristics you have learned about a person from talking to them. An example might be that they have mentioned to you that they planned on going to the gym more often. You could use this as an opportunity the next time you speak to notice that their arms look more toned than before. Your compliments should be genuine, as this is what will make people feel the best and will make them realize that you do care.

You should also be sure to remember special occasions and events that people have going on in their lives. If they tell you that they are going on a vacation or that their brother is getting married, you can remember these dates to bring them up later. It makes people feel special when you remember details about their lives, so do not just pass over them. They also did not mention them to you to be forgotten, and many people want you to remember what is going on in their life. When you make people feel remembered and show you have an interest in them, they can be easily influenced.

Showing interest in others can also be as simple as starting a conversation with them. Do not be afraid to follow up with someone after talking to them and do not show fear of being the first one to reach out. You need to make it clear that you want to know more about that person and that you care about your connection with them. Some people are afraid of being the first to contact the other, but you show power and courage in doing so.

You should also give well-thought-out feedback to people to show your interest. This is accomplished somewhat by complimenting but is not always the same. Providing feedback offers your general thoughts on something, as opposed to just the positive opinions or observations you have. You need to think about what other people tell you and judge when they want your opinion on something. People often seek approval or guidance from the people they trust, so it is a good sign if you are at this point with them. Be honest with them about your thoughts on each matter, but know your limits as well. Many people respect honesty, but you do not want to be so blunt that you hurt their feelings. Your feedback needs to be both considerate and honest so that the other person is appreciative instead of defensive.

Taking an interest in people mostly involves the respect that you show others. Everything we have learned in this chapter is what you should already be doing, but may be missing in your current interactions.

If you want to have an impact on what people do, you need to make an impact on their emotions first. No one will listen to you if you mean very little to them or do not show any interest in their lives. The point of this chapter is to help you show others that you do care and that you listen to their desires and what is going on in their lives.

Hopefully, by now, you have identified a few ways to go about showing an interest in other people, as well as the many other ways to involve people and their lives. All of this will help you to influence them because they will pick up on the efforts that you have shown them.

Chapter 8: Summary of Steps

This book has covered the seven most important steps to learning how to influence people. To be successful, it is important that you re-read these steps as needed and practice them often.

This chapter is meant to serve as a quick guide for you. Each step will be covered and given a small summary for your benefit.

Step 1: Having confident body language. This first step is meant to help you look the part and be confident.

Start by keeping your head, push out your chest, pull your stomach in, and keep your shoulders back. Monitor any non-purposeful movements you might be doing and maintain eye contact.

Body language is the first impression you give someone, so be sure that this step is always one of the first things you consider when trying to be influential.

Step 2: Make people like you. This step sounds easy enough, and you might already be good at accomplishing this.

If you need some help with making people like you, do not worry. You can start by being more charismatic. Do not be afraid to take control in a room and show that you care. People will respect you and enjoy being around you. It also will not hurt to make a joke every now and then as well.

Being humble will also start to make others like you, so do not forget to show humility now and again.

Step 3: Be clear and concise. You want people to understand your message and take out any guesswork.

Articulate what you want to say by taking out long, complicated words and get straight to the point. Make sure you use as many active verbs as possible and do not use vague nouns and words to send a message or ask a favor.

You also want to consider what you are going to say before you say it. This will help to make your message more concise after you have simplified it. You should also be sure to start and end with the main point. Keep supporting details to a minimum and include them in the middle of your overall message.

Step 4: Ask for favors. Use the principles of the "Ben Franklin Effect" to get people to do what you ask of them.

By getting people to agree to do small favors for you, you can also get them to do larger favors for you afterward.

You can also get people to do what you want by asking for it in an appropriate way. Be considerate of the other person and plan to ask at a time that works for them. You also want to be polite and make your intentions clear.

Do not be afraid to ask a favor of someone, but also be prepared for them to decline your favor.

Step 5: Make emotional connections. Sometimes it is not enough to have people like you to get them to do what you want. You need to work on building meaningful relationships with them, especially if you want long-lasting success in having influence over them.

You can do this by having strong conversations with people and by building rapport with them. You want them to talk about themselves and their experiences so that you can learn more about them. Once you know a lot about them, you can bring up what is going on in their life and show that you have been paying attention to what they have told you.

Step 6: Be more transparent. You want people to know who you are and not have to guess about your life. Do not be afraid to share about yourself or any emotions you have.

Being transparent will require you to be more vulnerable and open up to people. You want to be honest with them and show that they can trust you. They will also feel like they know you much better, which will be an important factor in getting them to listen to you.

Step 7: Take an interest in others. Do not be afraid to get to know people and pay attention to their lives. People love to feel special and as though you care about what they say.

Give compliments and feedback to people when warranted. Do not be afraid to reach out to them to talk or meet up, as this shows that you care. You want people to feel remembered, and showing an interest in their lives will accomplish this.

If you feel like you have missed any part of these steps, feel free to go back and read the chapter again. Each suggestion and tip can bring you closer to getting people to listen to you, so it is important that you understand each concept well.

Once you have reviewed each step, you are ready to do it on your own. Good luck and enjoy your newly found influence over others!

Conclusion

Thank you for making it through to the end of this book, let's hope it was informative and able to provide you with all of the tools you need to achieve your goals, whatever they may be.

The next step is to put the 7 steps into practice so that you may begin to influence the people around you. By learning and practicing each of the steps given in this book you will easily gain control over others and can make them do just about anything you want.

You have learned new skills, such as improving body language and how to make emotional connections, so that you can influence other people. It is now up to you to demonstrate your learned skills and get people to do what you want. This is no easy task, but soon you will be a professional at getting others to do your bidding.

Yes, it takes a lot of practice to master the different ways to influence people. You will find being able to influence – and manipulate – others can be very beneficial especially if you are someone that needs to show dominance over others. Of course, how you want to influence others will completely depend on you. You can be someone with positive influence to your peers or you can be someone who's very manipulative to others.

Finally, if you found this book useful in any way, your honest review on Amazon is always appreciated.

More by Dean Mack

Discover all books from the Social Skills Best Seller Series by Dean Mack at:

bit.ly/dean-mack

Book 1: *How to Flirt*

Book 2: *How to Start a Conversation*

Book 3: *How to Talk to People*

Book 4: *How to Ask Questions*

Book 5: *How to Be Funny*

Book 6: *How to Influence People*

Book 7: *How to Attract Men*

Book 8: *How to Attract Women*

Themed book bundles available at discounted prices:

bit.ly/dean-mack

9 798869 374615

Printed by Libri Plureos GmbH in Hamburg,
Germany